SIMPLY JEWISH

AN ILLUSTRATED, GET-TO-THE-POINT GUIDE TO JUDAISM

RABBI REUVEN EPSTEIN

Published by K'hal Publishing
111 John Street • Suite 1720
New York, NY 10038
212.791.7450

Printed in Canada by Kromar Printing Ltd.

SIMPLY JEWISH

AN ILLUSTRATED, GET-TO-THE-POINT
GUIDE TO JUDAISM

DEDICATED IN MEMORY OF

MILTON SHEDLIN z"l

A passionate man who believed that through
the joys of Jewish life, an enlightened and
inspired Jewish community would unfold.

He led a simple life grounded in
honesty, integrity and faith.

His legacy continues to grow through
the inspired efforts he has nurtured.

May his memory be blessed

In Honor of
Rabbi Doniel Staum, Rabbi Chaim Schabes,
Rabbi Yisroel Saperstein, and our good friend
Reuven Epstein, for maintaining a wonderful
spirit of brotherhood and love of Torah
in our community.

Mutty & Miriam Reznick

———

Dedicated to

The Tanenbaum family
of Augusta, Georgia

By Robert & Michelle Rothman & family,
New Hempstead, New York
Grandchildren of Minnie Tanenbaum,
great grandchildren of Hill & Miriam Yehudis
Tanenbaum, great-great grandchildren of
Chaim Gedaliah & Rivka Tanenbaum
and Jacob Beryl & Dora Tanenbaum

———

In Memory of

Chaya Renana Galit Hirschhorn

———

In Memory of

Paul Steinberg

———

In Memory of

David Taubenfeld

———

In Memory of

Aliza Raskin

———

In Memory of

Yisroel Yaakov (YY) Epstein

In Memory of

Morris and Goldie Kalter

My earliest memories of my father,
Rabbi Mosha Yaakov Epstein are of him sitting and learning.
As a Rabbi and Torah scholar he thirsts for more knowledge and
ways to impart it to the Jewish community. My brother follows
in those lofty footsteps. It is their values and leadership that have
inspired this dedication.

Juda J. and Anne Epstein

ACKNOWLEDGMENTS

First and foremost, I must express my tremendous gratitude to the Almighty, for all His blessings, and in particular for granting me the privilege of authoring this book.

As a first-time author, I thought that writing a book was merely a longer version of writing an article. During the past two years I have learned that many more steps are involved, and many people add tremendous value to the final product. I am deeply indebted to and would like to thank each of them.

Josh Penzell, whose probing questions during and especially after a Birthright trip to Israel, convinced me of the need for this type of book. Josh also reviewed the manuscript and had excellent questions and comments throughout.

Rabbi Dave Felsenthal and Israel Free Spirit, for sending me on these important Birthright trips.

My brother Rabbi Donneal Epstein, my uncle Rabbi Mendel Epstein, Rabbi Lawrence Hajioff, Rabbi Yisroel Ciner, Rabbi Yisroel Saperstein, Rabbi Yaakov Spivak, and Rabbi Yamin Goldsmith, for their guidance, review of the manuscript, and assistance with citations of Jewish law and sources.

Felicia Taubenfeld, Shoshana Schechter, Sam Shiel, Eve Lieberman, Michael Kats, and Anne Epstein, for their review of the manuscript and words of encouragement. Special thanks to my brother Yudi Epstein and to Zvi Raskin for their detailed review of the very raw first manuscript.

Rabbi Raphael Butler of The Afikim Foundation, a visionary involved in many important and inspiring projects. I am truly humbled that Rabbi Butler deemed this project worthy of his time and effort.

Rabbi Shimon Apisdorf, the accomplished author of the Rosh Hashanah Yom Kippur Survival Kit, and other excellent books, for providing the guidance necessary to make this book a reality.

Sharon Goldinger of PeopleSpeak for editing the manuscript in a way that truly captures the essence of what I mean to convey.

Karen Hochberg and Gitty Schachter of Afikim for their review and management of this project.

Rabbi Maier Feinberg, for serving as our fact checker.

Jamie Geller who has graciously allowed the use of several recipes from her popular book, Quick & Kosher: Recipes From the Bride Who Knew Nothing.

Peter Juricek for his efforts in taking and locating pictures. Sam Heineman of Quality Photography for allowing the use of several excellent wedding photos. Devorah Goldman for allowing the use of several excellent food- related photos from Quick & Kosher.

Levi Blumenfeld, for his tremendous efforts in selecting the appropriate photos, and in designing the book. If a picture is worth a thousand words, Levi's pictures are worth ten thousand words!

My holy teachers, my father, Rabbi Mosha Epstein, chief among them.

My students, who have inspired me far more than I could ever inspire them.

My wonderful children, Avi, Elisheva, Daniella, Michal, and Dovid. I appreciate their patience during the books long gestation period and the great enthusiasm they continue to have for it. But most of all

I appreciate them for being the fine young people they are. Special thanks to Elisheva for typing large portions of the initial draft.

My in-laws, Chaim and Freda Shiel of Toronto, Canada, for their help, guidance, love, and support.

My parents, Rabbi Mosha and Roslyn Epstein of Bridgeport, Connecticut. I was blessed to have such exemplary role models as parents. Instead of lectures about kindness, my parents had an unending parade of guests at their Shabbos table and in their home. Although my mother worked full time as a social worker, eventually becoming the director of a large city program, she was still a devoted mother and wife, a great hostess and the consummate Rebbetzin. My father would invite guests almost as fast as my mother could prepare for them. My father studied the Talmud at all hours, and his devotion to Torah study had a profound impact on all five of his children. If my father was not studying, he was at the synagogue, teaching, or visiting patients at the hospital or the home for the elderly. My father was my first teacher, and for many years my brother Yudi and I studied the Talmud with our father every day. My father wrote his own book, an important work dealing with proper Jewish burial, The Tahara Manual of Practices. Whatever positive deeds I have accomplished, have been a result of the example provided by my parents. May this book serve as a source of merit for my father's speedy recovery.

Last, but certainly not least, my beloved wife, Susan. As Rabbi Akiva famously told his students regarding his wife, "My Torah and your Torah are due to her" Ketuvot 62(b). Susan has always encouraged my studying, teaching, and writing. The warmth that fills our home is a reflection of her warmth. May she be blessed with true nachas from our children.

Reuven Epstein

SIMPLY JEWISH

AN ILLUSTRATED, GET-TO-THE-POINT GUIDE TO JUDAISM

Contents

How to Make a "Shiva Call"
What is "Kaddish"?
The "Unveiling"
Yartzeit/ Anniversary of the Date of Passing
Yizkor

Shabbat: All or Nothing?
How to Turn Friday Night Into Shabbat
The Shabbat Checklist
How to Light Shabbat Candles
Understanding Candle Lighting
Shalom Alaychem
Ayshet Chayil
Blessing the Children
Understanding "Blessing the Children"
Kiddush
How to Say Kiddush
How to Wash for Challah (or Bread)
Hamotzee: The Blessing on Challah
Fresh Hot Challah!
The Festive Shabbat Meal
Zmeerot: Singing at the Shabbat Table
The D'var Torah; Sharing Words of Torah
"Grace after Meals", Birkat Hamazon
Shabbat Morning
Havdalah: Shabbat's Closing Ceremony
Making the Shabbat Holy

Passover
The Passover Story
The Fast of The Firstborn
How to Make a Seder
Things You Will Need in Advance
Items Needed For the Seder Plate
Understanding the Seder Plate
'Taking' the Afikomen
The Seder
Rosh Hashanah
How to 'Do' Rosh Hashanah
Yom Kippur
How to 'Do' Yom Kippur
Sukkot
Shmini Atzeret and Simchat Torah

CHAPTER FOUR:

CHAPTER FIVE:

CHAPTER SIX:

PART 2

CHAPTER NINE:
Ready-To-Use Resources *149*

FOREWORD

Simply Jewish: a catchy title, perhaps, but there is, in reality, nothing simple about it. The complex inter-connectivity of Torah law and tradition that governs every aspect of our experience demands a work of greater depth and analysis. At the same time, there is a pattern of Jewish life, bound in the beauty of observance that in its totality creates the internal feel of living a life that is, in fact, Simply Jewish.

It is that heartbeat of the Jewish soul that we explore in an easily digested form creatively crafted by Rabbi Reuven Epstein and designed by Levi Blumenfeld. The life cycle experiences, the Jewish year of holidays and commemorations, the centrality of Israel to our faith and purpose, the meaning and value of mitzvot and customs, and the daily mantra of faith and observance, form the framework of a valued Jewish life.

The Afikim Foundation gratefully acknowledges the support of the Ministry of Religious Affairs, the World Zionist Organization and its Chairman, Avraham Duvdevani, in seeing that these enduring values continue to redound worldwide. As we go to press, the translation of this work has already begun, thus allowing this valued contribution to Jewish life to reach an ever-broadening world Jewish community.

The appellation Jew is an outgrowth of the name Judah, the regal son of Jacob. As the Torah recounts, prior to Jacob's exile into Egypt, he sent Judah ahead to establish houses of study and prayer. One of the commentaries explains that it is for that reason that we are called Jews, since our mission in life mirrors that of Judah; to establish opportunities of Jewish living anywhere we reside. This publication is a fulfillment of that charge. It is the first portal of entry for the inquisitive and searching. In its simplicity is its profundity.

We thank Rabbi Shimon Apisdorf, Maier Feinberg, Gitty Schachter and Karen Hochberg for their diligent review and management of this project. It is our hope that from these pages, a further enlightened and inspired community will grow.

Rabbi Raphael B. Butler
President, The Afikim Foundation
Iyar, 5771—May, 2011

INTRODUCTION

With all due apologies to Mr. Dickens, for Jews living in the United States, "it is the best of times, it is the worst of times". On one hand, Jews are more successful, and better educated than ever before. On the other hand, these same Jews are often unlettered in terms of knowledge of their own religion.

The main goal of this small book is to introduce Jewish rites, rituals and customs and to explain how to perform them. My philosophy is very simple. Whether you are a tenth generation Rabbi, or just found out that you are Jewish ten days ago, Judaism is your heritage! We are all equally entitled to practice its rich traditions.

A second goal of this book is to allow guests at traditional Jewish events and ceremonies to understand what they are experiencing. By necessity, each topic is discussed only briefly. In reality, we are barely scratching the surface. In fact, many of these topics have full volumes devoted exclusively to them, and many other topics are not mentioned at all. Nothing would please me more if you would use this book as a springboard to a more detailed study of our Faith. To facilitate additional study, I have included references to other, more detailed, materials.

How to Use This Book

This book is actually two books in one; Part I, Chapters 1-8, and Part II, the final chapter. In Part I, you will be introduced to Jewish rites, rituals, and customs and I will explain how they are performed. I have included "Insider" and "Understanding" sections to provide greater insights. The first time a Hebrew term is used it is explained, and all Hebrew terms are defined in the glossary. The chapters are organized in a way that will hopefully provide you with an intuitive method of locating desired topics quickly, requiring only the ability to determine if the desired topic is a "lifecycle event" or pertains to the "Shabbat" or "Holidays" and so on.

Prayers that appear in the main body of the book are in English. Pronunciation of Hebrew terms follows the pronunciation most commonly used in Israel today (For example, using the "t" sound instead of the "s" sound, resulting in words like "Shabbat", instead of "Shabbos"). In writing the explanations and definitions, I have attempted to be as faithful to Jewish laws/ Halachot and customs as much as possible. I have attempted to differentiate between normative practice and customs.

Part II is both a concise, user-friendly guide to common practices and ceremonies as well as a "mini prayer book." In Part I you will become familiar with the gamut of Jewish concepts, rituals, holidays, practices, lifecycle events and more. Then, Part II will equip you to actually perform the rituals, if so inclined. To facilitate easy use, all prayers and ceremonies in the appendices are in Hebrew, English, and are "transliterated" (the Hebrew blessing is written in English in a way that sounds like you are reading the blessing in Hebrew.)

PART 1

CHAPTER ONE:

Lifecycle Events

From birth to death, Judaism has many rituals;
let's explore them together.

WE ARE HAVING A BABY.

Mazel Tov! You have entered the hospital as two people and exited the hospital as three people. You are a partner with no less than the Almighty Himself in the creation of another soul.

Bringing a baby into the world is one of, if not the most, joyous and awesome experiences of our entire lives. Of course, having a baby is not merely a tremendous joy. It is also a tremendous responsibility. Our job as parents include providing for the physical and financial needs of our children, as well as providing an unconditionally loving and nurturing environment, so that they may reach their full potential including their full spiritual potential. The job of a parent also includes the responsibility to provide children with a good "moral compass" and to teach them the difference between right and wrong. A good way to start is by giving the child a Jewish name.

Picking a Jewish Name for Your Baby

Why Do I Need to Give My Baby a Jewish Name?

In the finest of Jewish traditions, the question of why to give your baby a Jewish name is answered with another question: What is a name? Is it merely the source of identification, or is it more? According to Jewish tradition, names have tremendous importance. A name indicates the true essence of a person. According to Jewish tradition, parents are given a spirit of prophecy when selecting a name for their child. Giving your child a Jewish name is also the first opportunity for you to involve your baby in our faith, and will be a source of Jewish pride and Jewish self-identification. Finally, we should recall that one of the primary factors that influenced God to release the Jewish Nation from slavery in Egypt, was the way the Jews kept their Jewish names, (as if to say "we know we may be falling short in many ways, but we still identify ourselves as Jews and want to be Jewish").

How Do You Pick a Jewish Name for a Baby?

The good news is that you have the aforementioned "spirit of prophecy" working for you. The bad news is, you are blissfully unaware of this. So how do you go about making this important decision?

We follow certain guidelines. First, we try to name the child after a close relative that has passed away. The Sephardic custom is to name after living relatives. Although naming after the deceased honors the memory of the deceased, the intent is also to show that the child is a branch of the same tree and is here to continue the goal or mission of the deceased. Sephardic Jews are Jews that trace their lineage and customs to the Middle East and Spain. Ashkenazic Jews are from Eastern and Western Europe.

Even though we may not be aware of it, every person is meant to accomplish something in this world, "a mission". Yes, believe it or not, you are on a mission from God. Every family has a mission as well. These missions can be simple or complex. Sometimes they can be accomplished relatively quickly, and sometimes they can take several generations to complete. Did you ever wonder why you were born into the family you were? Was it coincidence, or the luck of the draw? Hardly. God gives each of us the tools we need to succeed in our personal missions and places us carefully within our specific families so that we may work towards our personal and family goals.

A second source of Jewish names is the Torah reading or holiday that coincides with the birth of the child. For example, one of my siblings has the middle name Mordechai because he was born shortly before the Purim holiday (see Chapter 5, holidays).

Finally, there are books of Jewish names, and I have listed some in the recommended sources, Chapter 9. We believe that a name is a portent for the future, so great care should be made to name the baby after a person of outstanding moral character or to select a name that has a positive, optimistic meaning. It's a bad idea to select a name that sounds "cool", if the originator of the name was a bad person.

Isn't This a Little Superstitious?

Every person has free will and has the free choice to be whatever type of person he or she wants to be. However, a child that is named Jacob and is called Jacob thousands of times, will eventually know he shares the name of our patriarch, and this can have a positive impact. A child given the name of Jacob's evil twin brother, Aysav, can expect the opposite.

Naming a Girl

When Do You Name a Baby Girl?

The naming of a girl is done during the Torah reading in synagogue. The Torah is read on Shabbat and on Monday and Thursday mornings. One custom is to specifically try and name the baby the very first time the Torah is read following her birth, demonstrating our eagerness

to perform mitzvot. The other custom is to wait until the Shabbat Torah reading for the naming ceremony. Both customs are perfectly acceptable.

How Do You Name a Baby Girl?

The father is given an "aliyah", meaning he is "called up" to the Torah, and recites the standard blessing recited whenever we read the Torah. In addition to the standard Torah blessing, prayers are added for the health of the mother and the baby, both of whom may still be in the hospital. At this point, we recite the short prayer in which the baby girl is given her Jewish name. All in attendance say "Mazel Tov". It is also customary for the parents to sponsor a "kiddush" (refreshments for the Congregation), after the Sabbath service, as a way of showing gratitude to God. Typically, this is done a few weeks after the birth because we wait for the mother to be able to comfortably attend. The kiddush may be formal or informal, large or small. I have attended formal sit down kiddushes that closely resembled wedding banquets, and informal kiddushes where only sponge cake and herring were served.

Isn't My Daughter Getting the Short End of the Stick Compared to the Bris My Son Had?

My son once made a similar observation to his twin sister. First, it should be noted that nothing prevents you from making your daughter's kiddush as formal and festive as your son's bris. As I told my son in my daughter's presence, "I guess she was just perfect the way she was born".

We believe that men and women are equal, and that neither sex is better than the other. However, that does not mean we have the same roles. The Torah contains 613 mitzvot and no one person can do them all. Some mitzvot apply only to men, some only to women, some only to rich people, some to poor, some only to the king, some only to a judge in court and some only in the land of Israel, some only outside the land of Israel. We are being given a message. We all have our roles, and should certainly accomplish the mitzvot that we can. If we aspire to fulfill the entire Torah, we should recognize that we can only do so in partnership with others.

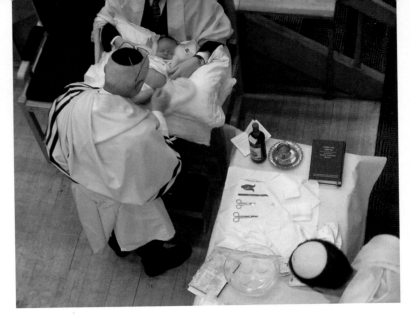

"BRIS"/CIRCUMCISION

In Biblical times, God commanded Abraham (Genesis 17:11) to personally have a circumcision; and commanded that on the eighth day of a boy's life, his foreskin be circumcised.

A 'Bris' is a great and joyous event, because it brings the baby into the 'covenant' of Abraham. Bris is the Hebrew word for covenant. Preferably, the Bris takes place in the morning, symbolizing our eagerness to perform the mitzvot. The health of the baby is always the primary concern, and therefore if the baby is not well, the circumcision is delayed. During the actual circumcision, 'the Gates of Heaven' are open, making it an especially appropriate time for prayer.

According to tradition, bringing the baby into the room where the Bris is performed, and passing him to the 'sandek', is the source of merit for couples attempting to have children. The sandek is the person holding the baby during the circumcision. It is a great honor to be the sandek, and according to tradition, a source of material blessing. The parents of the baby decide in advance whom they wish to perform which honors. The person who actually performs the circumcision is called the 'mohel'. When the baby is placed on the lap of the sandek, the mohel recites the following blessing:

"Blessed are You, Ado-noy, our God, King of the Universe, Who has made us holy with His commandments, and commanded us concerning circumcision".

Simply Jewish

The father recites the following blessing:

"Blessed are You, Ado-noy*, our God, King of the Universe, Who has made us holy with His commandments, and commanded us to bring him (this baby) into the covenant of our father Abraham".

Then, all present respond:

Just as he has entered into the covenant, may he also enter into Torah, into marriage and into good deeds.

*"ADO-NOY"- is one of the holy names of God, and throughout this book, it is hyphenated out of respect; but when you say it, it should be pronounced without hyphenation.

After a few more short blessings, the baby is given his "Jewish name". Just as parents give much thought to the selection of a child's legal name, they should choose a Jewish name with appropriate deliberation, because we believe that the child will carry that Jewish name forever. The full text for the ceremony is reproduced in Hebrew, English and spelled phonetically in Chapter 9.

PIDYAN HA-BEN/ REDEEMING YOUR OLDEST SON

What Is a Pidyan Ha-Ben?

"Pidyan Ha-Ben", redeeming your oldest son, is a Biblical mitzvah; (Exodus 13:1-15, Numbers 3:11-13, 44-48). When the Children of Israel were enslaved in Egypt, God subjected the Egyptians to ten plagues, the last of which was the death of their firstborn. Since God spared the firstborn of the Children of Israel, they became holy. The verse states that to redeem the oldest son, you must pay five shekel to the priest.

I'm Pretty Traditional, How Come I've Never Heard of This?

As a practical matter, the Pidyan Ha-ben ceremony occurs less frequently than you might expect. It occurs only when the firstborn is male, born via natural delivery (the verse specifies "opens the womb") to a Jewish woman who has not yet had children, nor a miscarriage or abortion, and only if both parents are not from the two priestly groups, Kohen and Levy.

How Is It Done?

The mitzvah is to redeem the firstborn son after thirty days. As a way of demonstrating our eagerness to perform mitzvot, the redemption should occur on the thirty first day following the birth, unless that day is Shabbat or a holiday. Once it is confirmed that the mitzvah of redemption applies, the parents should select the Kohen from whom they will redeem their son. This is not as simple as it appears. Not every Cohen is a Kohen. We prefer someone who has a longstanding tradition of being from a family known to be Kohanim. Additionally, since the Kohen will be bestowing a blessing upon your son, it would be prudent to try and choose an especially righteous individual to impart the blessing. You will also need the "five shekel" in advance. Since we understand the verse to refer to silver coins, we typically use five silver dollars. Paper money, checks, credit cards, even coins that are devoid of silver, may not be used.

The Kohen, the family, the baby, and invited guests, assemble. The redemption commences with the father declaring that both he and his wife are not from priestly families and that this child is their firstborn child. The baby is then handed to the Kohen. The Kohen then asks, "Do you prefer your oldest son, or the five shekel you would be required to redeem him with"? Hopefully, the Dad will pick the baby. The entire ceremony is reproduced in Chapter 9. After the redemption has been completed, family and friends enjoy a festive meal.

Pidyan Ha-Ben "Insider"

If a man was never redeemed as a baby, he has the mitzvah to redeem himself, regardless of his age. It is also possible for the same father to make more than one Pidyan Ha-ben if he had firstborn sons with more than one woman.

UPSHERIN

What Is an Upsherin?

"Upsherin" is a Yiddish term meaning "cutting off". Some have the custom to wait until a boy's third birthday to give him his first haircut. This custom is believed to have originated with the Kabbalists, and later popularized in the Chasidic communities. Today, outside of

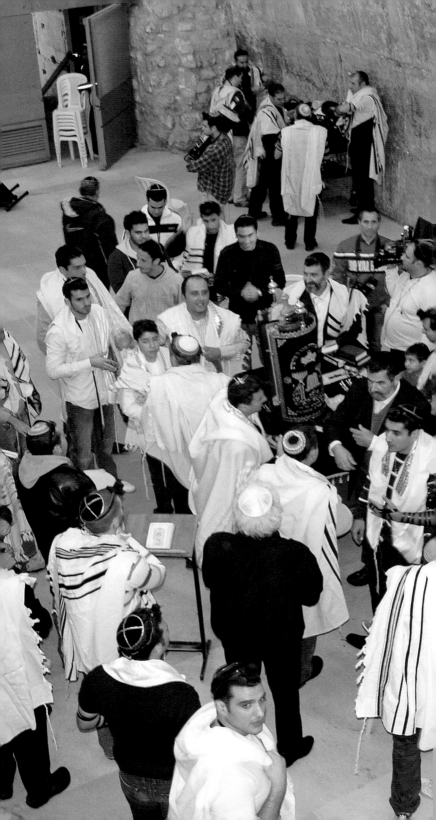

Chasidic and some Sephardic communities, it is not normative practice to wait three years to give a boy his first haircut, although there are exceptions.

How Is It Done?

On the baby's third birthday, family and friends assemble. They take turns snipping strands of hair and bestowing blessings upon the child. This is also considered an ideal time to introduce the child to ritual observance and Torah study. He is given a Kippa and Tzitzit, (actually a Talit Katan). As part of this ceremony, the child may also be introduced to the "aleph-bet", the Jewish alphabet. Additionally, some families weigh the hair that was cut off and donate a corresponding amount to charity.

BAT MITZVAH AND BAR MITZVAH

A young lady upon attaining her 12th birthday and a young man upon his 13th birthday are recognized as adults, regarding the performance of Jewish laws and customs. The "Bat" (daughter), and "Bar" (son) Mitzvah rituals are meant to mark the coming of age and becoming part of the Jewish People. (Girls attain adulthood earlier because they mature earlier than boys.)

A festive, celebratory meal acknowledging this milestone, is appropriate and important. In truth, however, it is a little anticlimactic, because in the eyes of Jewish law it happens automatically whether the ceremony is lavish, simple, or non-existent. Even more important than the celebratory meal is making sure that the day includes some type of undertaking by the Bar or Bat Mitzvah that demonstrates that he or she is becoming part of the community.

Historically, some of the following have been included:
- Delivering a Bar or Bat Mitzvah Speech.
- A special meal with family and friends.
- Reading the weekly Torah reading.
- Chanting the Haftorah, (the Haftorah is the weekly reading from the book of prophets that is connected to the Torah reading).
- Leading a prayer service.
- Being called to the Torah to recite the blessings.

While it remains admirable and appropriate to perform these rituals, if you attend a Sabbath Bar Mitzvah you are likely to see some combination of them. A newer trend has been for young people to be involved in an important Jewish project, such as working in a soup kitchen and collecting and distributing toys for hospitalized children or for children in Israel. This project becomes part of the Bar/Bat Mitzvah celebration.

Take on specific mitzvahs, such as making Kiddush Friday night; or lighting Shabbat candles.

To be candid, as an old Hebrew school teacher and principal, Bar/ Bat Mitzvahs elicit mixed feelings. On the one hand, I am truly happy that this young person has come of age, and I am proud of what he or she accomplished on this special day. On the other hand, I know that statistically speaking, this day that is supposed to represent the beginning of communal Jewish involvement, often marks the end of communal Jewish involvement.

Ways to Make the Bar or Bat Mitzvah More Meaningful

Here are some tips for parents on how to make the special day more meaningful:

1. Sure, make it a nice party, but try to make one that is less 'bar' and more mitzvah.
2. Talk to your child in advance about the idea of 'coming of age', of becoming a part of the Jewish community and why that is important.
3. Consider having your child participate in one of the more traditional rituals, if that is in their skill set. Even if your child knows how to read Hebrew, reading the Torah properly will require a great deal of effort, all the more so, if your child does not read Hebrew. Reading the phonetically spelled blessing when called to the Torah will require much less effort.
4. Have your child and his or her classmates participate in a meaningful communal project.
5. Finally, please make sure your child knows this is meant to be the beginning, not the end.

What to Expect At a Jewish Wedding

If you've never been to a Jewish wedding, you may be puzzled by what you see. Here are some questions you might have.

"It's their wedding and it's only an hour before the ceremony, why aren't the bride and groom together?"

It's a longstanding custom that the bride and groom do not see each other the week prior to their wedding. On the day of the wedding, they greet their guests, but in separate rooms.

"How come the bride and groom are not eating any hors d'oeuvres?"

Another custom is for the bride and groom to fast on their wedding day until after the ceremony. Why? Because the wedding day is a little like Yom Kippur, it is a new beginning. According to tradition, God forgives the sins of the bride and groom and they start their new life together with a clean slate.

Before the actual wedding ceremony is the 'Badeckin', the placing of the veil on the bride. The groom, who had been sitting with his father, his father-in-law, and other friends and relatives, is literally 'danced' into the main reception area. In the reception area the bride awaits, sitting majestically, as if on a throne, flanked by her mother, her mother-in law, and most of the other guests. This is often a very special moment, as the young couple have not seen each other for an entire week. A veil is placed over the face of the bride and the groom is escorted out. The origins of the Badeckin can be traced to our forefather Jacob. Jacob was famously fooled into thinking that the veiled woman he married was Rachel. We want the groom to be sure who it is under the veil.

The Ceremony

At the ceremony, both the bride and the groom typically wear white. It is traditional for the groom to wear a 'kitel' during the ceremony. The kitel is the same white robe worn during the high holidays, as this is another indication that the wedding day is likened to a private Yom Kippur.

The parents of the groom escort him down the aisle to the canopy or 'Chuppah'. The parents of the bride do the same. This is meant to symbolize the willingness of the parents to "let go" and allow their relationship with their child to be superseded by the marital relationship in fulfillment of the verse, "and man shall leave his parents and cling to his wife"; (Genesis 2:24).

The custom, when feasible, is to have the wedding ceremony outside, under the stars. This is to remember God's blessing to Abraham that his children will be "as numerous as the stars". Symbolically, we bestow this same blessing upon the new couple. A wedding hall that is used for traditional weddings, may well have a small sky roof that is opened during the ceremony.

The Ketubah

Often hand-made by an artist; and later beautifully framed, the Ketubah is an ornate document that is read aloud in Hebrew. Most people have no idea what is being read. Sorry to dash any romantic notions, but the "Ketubah" is a contract. It specifically spells out the groom's obligation to the bride, including his obligation to support her. Romance is great, but Judaism is also concerned about rights and obligations.

The Chuppah (Canopy)

The ceremony itself takes place under the Chuppah. The Chuppah is a large rectangular cloth canopy supported by four poles. The Chuppah is meant to symbolize the new home being built.

The Bride Circles the Groom

Under the Chuppah, the bride circles the groom seven times. There are many mystical reasons given for this. One reason is that, just as Joshua circled Jericho seven times and the walls fell down, so too, after seven circles any barriers between the new couple should fall. Another reason for the bride to circle the groom is so that wherever he looks, he should only see his wife; and he should understand from this point onward he must "only have eyes" for her.

The Ring

The heart of the ceremony is when the groom gives his bride the ring and says (or repeats after the Rabbi) the Hebrew version of "You are consecrated to me according to the laws of Moses and Israel." During a traditional ceremony only the groom gives a ring to the bride.

The Blessings

Seven blessings are recited under the Chuppah at this stage of the wedding, (see Chapter 9 for the full text of the seven blessings or "sheva brachot"). Different family members or distinguished rabbis are

often called up to recite the blessings. Included are blessings that the young couple be happy, have a great family, and build a meaningful life together. After the last of the blessings the bride and groom both drink from the same goblet, symbolizing their now shared lives.

Jerusalem of Glass

Immediately after the completion of the blessings, a glass is placed on the ground and the groom breaks it with his foot. What an odd thing to do at such a happy moment. But that is exactly the point. Even though this is such a joyous moment in their lives, the young couple, and all present, are reminded that our Temple

was destroyed and that we, the Jewish People, are still in exile.

As the glass is broken; the band starts to play and everyone shouts "Mazel Tov" or "Good Luck".

The young couple is serenaded by guests, and they are joyously escorted out of the wedding

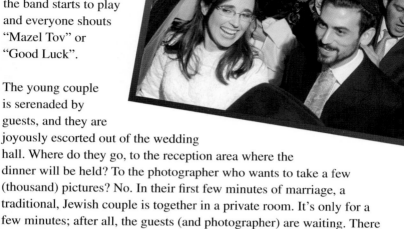

hall. Where do they go, to the reception area where the dinner will be held? To the photographer who wants to take a few (thousand) pictures? No. In their first few minutes of marriage, a traditional, Jewish couple is together in a private room. It's only for a few minutes; after all, the guests (and photographer) are waiting. There are different (Halachic/ Jewish law) reasons for this, but one idea is that from here on, they must put each other first.

Does Judaism Permit Divorce?

Not infrequently, I am asked if Jewish law allows for divorces. (I assume that the Catholic Church's anti-divorce policy is the source for this confusion). Judaism does allow for divorce. It is explicitly authorized in the Torah, Deuteronomy 24:1, but there are two important caveats.

One, divorce was meant as the remedy of last resort for truly untenable situations. Divorce was not meant to be the means of ending literally fifty percent of all marriages, as it sadly is today. As it says in the Talmud, when a couple divorces "even the altar weeps"; (Sanhedrin 22a).

Two, for the divorce to be effective in ending the marriage, formal requirements must be met. For example, the document (or 'Get' in Hebrew) must be written by a scribe, on parchment, stating the full names of the parties, and where they reside. It must be signed by two appropriate witnesses, and the 'Get' must be worded in a way that it unconditionally ends the marriage. A divorce that does not meet the formal requirements poses a barrier to remarriage.

We would all rather focus on the more joyous lifecycle events, but eventually everyone must deal with death and mourning. Judaism has much to offer on the topic.

A Time to Live, A Time to Die

Some Basic Jewish Beliefs About Death

Every human being is a combination of a body and a soul, which God Himself has bestowed upon the individual. The moment of death is the time when the soul departs the body.

One of the main tenets of Judaism is that death is not the end. It marks the beginning of a new existence in the "World of Souls". Furthermore, we believe that in the times of the Messiah, in the "World to Come", the souls will return and once again be reunited with their bodies. (For a more detailed description see *Remember My Soul*, by Lori Palatnik).

From the moment of death until the time of burial, the soul hovers above the body. During this time the soul is very confused, because it is very difficult to comprehend this complete shift in existence. The soul is aware of all that happens around the body. The body should not be left alone during this difficult period. Additionally, great care should be taken to treat the body in a respectful manner.

A Jewish burial society, called a "Chevra Kadisha" helps in caring for the deceased, and performs the "Tahara", the washing and purifying of the body. After the Tahara, the body is dressed in plain white shrouds. (For more information regarding the Tahara process and the working of the burial societies, see *Tahara Manual of Practices*, by Rabbi Mosha Epstein).

Judaism strictly prohibits cremation because it is a desecration of the body, and the body, host of your soul and true essence, retains its holiness even after death. The only acceptable method of caring for the body after death is to bury it in the ground in fulfillment of the verse, "from the ground you have come and to the ground you shall return"; (Genesis 3:19).

What to Expect at a Jewish Funeral

As mentioned in the previous section, the time between death and burial is a very difficult one for the deceased. Thus, every effort should be made to have the funeral and burial as quickly as possible. The idea of a wake or a visitation where the deceased is dressed up and lies in repose in an opened casket for viewing is very foreign to Judaism. The funeral is meant to be simple and brief. Essentially it has three components. It starts with appropriate passages from Psalms, almost always including Psalm 120; which includes the verse, "though I walk in the valley of the shadow of death, I fear not."

The next component of a Jewish funeral is the offering of eulogies. Eulogies are given by close relatives, the Rabbi of the deceased, or an officiating Rabbi, and depending on the number of other speakers, a close friend or two. There is no right or wrong number of eulogies or a set length for a eulogy. However, a short heartfelt eulogy is often better received than a longer one. The purpose of the eulogy is to try to capture the essence and the good qualities of the departed. The soul of the departed is in attendance and is listening as well. The soul is comforted by appropriate eulogies and pained by poor eulogies. It is even more pained by untrue eulogies.

The final part of the Jewish funeral is the brief memorial prayer, the "Ail Malay", asking God to bring this soul "under the... wings of Your Divine Presence. And let this soul be bound up in the bond of eternal life".

At the end of the funeral the casket is led out, followed first by the family and then by all those assembled for the funeral.

Attendance at the burial is also a great mitzvah. Even if you are unable to attend the burial, 'accompanying' the casket for at least 6 feet, symbolically accompanying the deceased on this last trip, is important.

Indeed, all efforts extended on behalf of the deceased, from caring for the body, to participating in the burial, and everything in between, are deemed to be in a special category of mitzvot, called "chesed shel emet", or "true kindness". Why? Because many of the favors or good deeds we do for people may be tinged with some degree of self interest. Kindness to the deceased is done without any expectation of reciprocation and is therefore considered "true kindness".

"Mourners" include the parents of the deceased, children, siblings and spouse. At the completion of the burial, the mourners' garments are torn, as a vivid sign of mourning, and they recite the "Mourner's Kaddish" for the first time. Kaddish is the special prayer recited by mourners for eleven months on the anniversary (yartzeit) of the passing. After Kaddish is recited, all the non-mourners divide into two lines, and as the mourners walk by, words of condolence are offered.

> **KINDNESS TO THE DECEASED IS CONSIDERED "TRUE KINDNESS".**

Upon their return to the Shiva house, the mourners are served the "meal of consolation", which should include (but does not have to be limited to) bread, eggs, and cooked lentils. (All "official" Jewish meals include bread, and the round shape of the eggs and lentils are meant to symbolize that life is a cycle).

What is "Sitting Shiva" and Who "Sits Shiva"?

'Shiva' is the seven day mourning period that commences with the day of burial. During this time, close relatives of the deceased, (parents, children, siblings, spouse) 'sit' in one place, typically their own home or the home of the deceased, and mourn their great loss. Judaism recognizes the need to grieve and wants to eliminate the temptation to immediately get back to life as if "everything is normal".

A common question is "Do I really have to sit Shiva for seven days?" Some people have adopted the practice of sitting Shiva for three days. First, to point out the obvious, the word "Shiva" is actually a Hebrew word that means "seven". Linguistics aside, Shiva should be observed for seven days for more substantive reasons. The first day of Shiva is the day of the burial, thus, only a brief amount of time is actually spent sitting Shiva. The last day of Shiva is also a partial day. So, if you are only sitting Shiva for three days, you would actually only be sitting Shiva for one full day. When we remember that Shiva is observed only for close relatives, one day is just not enough.

How to Sit Shiva

The mirrors in the Shiva house are covered. Grooming, including shaving, and putting on makeup, is not allowed, as the emphasis should not be on external appearances. Bathing is only permitted for basic hygiene and deodorant is allowed for the same reason. The mourners sit low to the ground, on stools or special short chairs, and they don't wear leather shoes, to symbolize their grief. The garment torn at the burial should be worn.

Friends and family make a 'Shiva call', visiting the mourners and comforting them by sharing meaningful memories of the deceased. Most of the symbols of mourning are removed after seven days, but some, (attending parties, for example), remain in place for 30 days. After the death of a parent, mourning is not complete for a full year. More detailed sources regarding the laws of mourning are listed in the Recommended Sources section.

It should be noted that Shiva is meant to be the time to reflect on your loss, to remember the true essence of your loved one, and to properly grieve. The restrictions, mandatory as they may be, are meant to assist in that process. Thus, to focus on the restrictions instead of on the mourning and reflection, would be putting the focus in the wrong place.

How to Make a "Shiva Call"

During the seven day period that follows burial, the mourners sit Shiva. During this time, family and friends visit the mourner to console them, and this visit is called a Shiva call.

Although it sounds very simple, making a Shiva call is becoming a bit of a lost art. I thought it would be helpful to try and distill the principles into a list.

When to Visit

Confirm where the family will be sitting and during what hours. It is appropriate for mourners to post on their front door the times they will be sitting Shiva. Many mourners find sitting Shiva surprisingly tiring so it would be inappropriate to visit later than they wish. Also note that there is no Shiva on the Sabbath, so there will be curtailed hours on Friday and no Saturday visits until after nightfall.

Generally, the first day or two of Shiva, when the family feels their loss most keenly and are likely to be most emotional, is an appropriate time for family and close friends to visit.

An especially good time to visit is during the time minyan (prayer service) is scheduled, especially if the family is worried about having enough people to say the Kaddish (see following section).

Shiva Etiquette

Walk into the Shiva house without ringing the bell.

Don't greet the mourners verbally, because they are prohibited from exchanging greetings during the mourning period.

Don't expect a 'deli platter' at the Shiva house. Traditionally, friends and family bring food into the Shiva house for practical reasons. Mourners are unable to go out to a store to buy food, and/or they don't have the ability to prepare meals for their family; therefore, food is brought in for the mourners and their households. This food was not meant to be for visitors making Shiva calls.

Don't overstay your welcome. Generally, a half hour visit is a good rule of thumb. If you are a close friend, or there are not many other visitors and you think your presence is helpful, staying longer is appropriate. On the other hand, if the Shiva house is "standing room only", and the next wave is walking in, leaving earlier to make room for the next visitors is appropriate.

What to Say During the Visit

The purpose of the Shiva call is to comfort the mourners. Ideally, this is accomplished through sharing meaningful memories of the deceased. Sometimes the mourners aren't able or willing to talk. Respect their wishes. Even if you sit down in complete silence, you have shown the mourners that you 'feel their pain', and this is a great comfort. Once a mourner has initiated conversation, it is appropriate to say simple words of consolation such as "I am sorry". Try to remember some positive deed or story about the deceased, especially if it's a story you don't think the family is aware of. What if your friend is sitting Shiva and you didn't really know the deceased? It would be appropriate to ask your friend about the life of the deceased.

What Not to Say During the Visit

Many a Shiva call has digressed into a discussion about sports or politics. This is inappropriate, because it is not the purpose of the visit. We believe that true comfort is accomplished by remembering the positive attributes of the deceased, not through distracting the mourner with pleasant, but idle chatter. Far worse is offending the mourner you seek to comfort, by saying the wrong thing. For example, a visitor tried to 'comfort' a young widow by telling her she was fortunate that she didn't have any children and was still young enough to marry again. Beyond such an obvious faux-pas, even more common and less offensive 'words of comfort' may not be well-received by all mourners. For example, telling a mother who has lost a child, "at least you have other children", is rarely comforting, because the existence of other children cannot lessen the tremendous pain of the loss of this child.

> "MAY GOD COMFORT YOU AMONG THE MOURNERS OF ZION AND JERUSALEM."

The main point is that it is important to use common sense and realize that every word you use should be measured. At a time when people feel tremendous pain, and are often more sensitive than they might otherwise be, be very careful not to add to that pain.

What to Say When Leaving

When leaving, it is customary to say the following, "May God comfort you among the mourners of Zion and Jerusalem". This blessing is typically posted in the house of mourning.

What is "Kaddish"?

Kaddish, or more precisely "The Mourner's Kaddish", is the short prayer first said by mourners immediately after burial. Kaddish is said throughout the Shiva week during the prayer services, and daily at the synagogue during the eleven months after the death of a parent, and on the 'yartzeit', the anniversary of the relative's passing.

The Mourner's Kaddish is not just a memorial prayer for the deceased. In fact, if you look at the text reproduced in Chapter 9, you will notice that the deceased, or even death, is not mentioned at all.
The Mourners' Kaddish is an affirmation by the mourner of God's justice and a universal prayer for peace and redemption.

Why is this type of prayer said now? What is it meant to accomplish? I think we can answer both of these questions with a story. Rabbi Akiva, one of the great sages of the Talmud, had a terrible dream in which the recently deceased tax collector was in great anguish. This was an era when tax collectors had great power, and this man had caused much trouble and was despised. Rabbi Akiva understood that the tax collector's predicament was caused by the bad deeds committed in his life and also understood that the one way to help him was to have good deeds done on his behalf. Rabbi Akiva found the tax collector's unlettered son and taught the boy how to read and how to say the Mourner's Kaddish. The tax collector soon returned to Rabbi Akiva's dreams and reported that his lot was much improved because the public sanctification of God through reciting the Kaddish is a merit to the soul of the deceased.

As the story demonstrates, saying Kaddish and prayers are helpful to the soul of the deceased, but they are not the main thing. " The principal thing is for the children to walk in the proper path, and when they do so, they obtain divine merit and grace for their parents", (Zohar). Children are an extension of their parents. Every good deed a child does counts as a good deed for both the child and the parent. (Alas, the opposite is true as well). The best thing we can do for a parent is to live good, moral, Jewishly connected lives.

The Unveiling

"The unveiling" is the ceremony at which the memorial stone that permanently marks the grave is unveiled. At this brief ceremony, Psalms and the "Ail Malay" prayer are recited. A relative or friend should share some thoughts about the deceased. The ceremony concludes with the family reciting Kaddish.

The memorial stone should state the name of the deceased, as well as the date of his or her passing. It has become the custom to include an appropriate descriptive thought or sentence that captures the essence of the deceased.

Far less appropriate is the phrase on each memorial stone in a particular section of a Long Island cemetery. It declares that the deceased "Lived to bowl", and includes a little bowling ball engraved on the stone. Now, I like to bowl as much as the next guy, but I hope that we can understand that it is a mere recreational activity and not our essence. Truth be told, those bowlers are an easy target, as they are an obvious example of people losing sight of what is truly important in life. If a person's memorial stone said "Lived to shop" with the local mall engraved on it, or "Lived to work" with a little picture of the office, would that be much better?

We should be aware that one day there will be a memorial stone for each and every one of us, and we, knowingly or unknowingly, are writing it. Wouldn't it be wise to think about what we want our memorial stone to look like, and then live a life that reflects those ideals?

Mourning, the End of the First Year, and Subsequent Years

The passage of time may diminish our sense of loss, but we never forget our departed love ones, nor should we. Jewish law recognizes the need to mourn, and later remember our close relatives, but it also balances it with the need to carry on with life. We specifically remember our close relatives on the anniversary of the date of their passing, the yartzeit, and during the Yizkor service.

Yartzeit

What Is a Yartzeit?

The yartzeit is the anniversary of the date of passing of a loved one. The term is derived from the combination of the Yiddish words for "year" and "time". The date is determined by the Jewish calendar. Therefore, even if you know your parent passed away on January 1st, due to fluctuations in the calendars, the yartzeit date can vary by several weeks. Yartzeit observance is another example of how we distinguish between parents and other close relatives. It is normative Jewish practice to observe the yartzeit of a parent, but merely a custom to observe the yartzeit of other close relatives.

How Is It Observed?

On the date of the yartzeit we recite kaddish and light a "yizkor" or "memorial" candle - a special candle that remains lit during the twenty four hour yartzeit. It is appropriate to fast on a parent's yartzeit, if that is possible. It is customary to visit the parent's grave. It is also customary to try and do as many positive deeds as possible because these deeds accrue to the benefit of your parents and help elevate their souls. Examples of this include studying Torah, giving charity, or performing other acts of kindness, (see Chapter 7 "The Three Pillars").

PERFORMING GOOD DEEDS ON BEHALF OF THEIR PARENTS, AS A MEANS OF ELEVATING THEIR SOULS.

Yizkor

What Is Yizkor?

Yizkor is the prayer recited by children to recall the memory of their departed parents. It is recited on Yom Kippur, Shavuot, Passover, and the end of Sukkot/Shmini Atzeret. Congregants who have not lost parents step outside during this prayer. It is traditional for children to pledge charity or undertake to perform good deeds on behalf of their parents, as a means of elevating their souls.

CHAPTER TWO:
Shabbat

What is the Sabbath?

To begin, let's clarify a little terminology. "The Sabbath", "Shabbat", and "Shabbos" are just slightly different terms for the same day. How could that happen? Shabbat is the Sephardic pronunciation, Shabbos is the Ashkenazic pronunciation, and Sabbath is the 'Anglicized' version. I will use the terms interchangeably.

The Sabbath is the period from sundown Friday until dark on Saturday. Many are tempted to define "Shabbat" as the time in which "Jews are prohibited from working and doing many other things". While it is technically true that work and other types of activities are prohibited on Shabbat, this is not the definition of the day, but rather only one of its characteristics.

First and foremost, the Sabbath is a holy day. It is the weekly commemoration of God's creating the universe in six days and resting on the seventh day. It is a day to take a break from the rat race. "Six days you shall work, but on the seventh day you shall rest"; (Exodus 20:9). It is a day to ignore telephones, cell phones, beepers, pagers, laptops, Blackberries, emails, text messages, and all other modern "conveniences" that make our lives easier, yet more complicated. It

is a day to spend with your children, (you know, the little guys you occasionally pass during the week). It is a day to spend with your better half. It is a spiritual day. It is the day of rest.

Yes, it is true that there are many laws and requirements. But it would be impossible to have a meaningful day of rest without restrictions. In other words, "More than the Jews have kept the Sabbath, the Sabbath has kept the Jews.", as Ahad Ha'am wrote. It is this weekly opportunity to rest and reconnect spiritually and with our family, that has retained the Jewish people throughout the millennia.

Shabbat is so central to Judaism that it is mentioned numerous times in the Bible and it is among the Ten Commandments.

Shabbat: All or Nothing?

On a recent Birthright trip to Israel, one of the young ladies told me that she was moved by the Friday night candle lighting. She wanted to start lighting every Friday night, yet she realized she was far from observant. She wanted to know whether it would be hypocritical to light Friday night candles and then go out for the evening.

The answer is that Shabbat is not all or nothing.

The Ten Commandments are written in the Torah/Bible two times. The wording is slightly different in each place, and the full text is in Chapter eight, The Three Pillars. One time the Torah says "Keep the Sabbath", and one time the Torah says, "Remember the Sabbath". "Remembering the Sabbath" instructs us to verbally mention the Sabbath and to mention its praise, this is done by reciting the Kiddush, (see below). Yes, it would be best to both "Keep" and "Remember" the Sabbath. But if today you can't keep the Sabbath, it is certainly appropriate to at least 'honor' the Sabbath by lighting candles and reciting the Kiddush, (see below), or doing whatever you can do.

How to Turn Friday Night Into Shabbat

Maybe you recently ate a Friday night meal at a friend's house or attended the excellent "Shabbat Across America" program (njop.org), and enjoyed it. Now you are wondering, can I possibly pull this off on my own? The answer is, of course you can.

To get started, here's a handy checklist. Each of these items will be covered in detail in this chapter:

The Shabbat Checklist

- Light Shabbat Candles
- Shalom Alaychem
- Ayshet Chayil/ Woman of Valor
- Bless the Children
- Kiddush
- Washing for Bread and Hamotzee, the Blessing for Bread
- Festive Meal
- Singing/Zmeerot
- Words of Jewish Wisdom/ D'var Torah
- Birkat Hamazon/ Grace After Meal

How to Light Shabbat Candles

Candle lighting is ideally done 18 minutes before sunset. It may be

done earlier. That would "bring in Shabbat earlier", which is certainly permissible. Candle lighting may not be done after sunset.

Typically, two candles are lit, although there is a custom to add one candle for each child. Almost any type of candles may be used, provided they don't flicker, don't have a bad odor and last for at least two hours. Today, wax candles are used almost exclusively.

Although we typically recite blessings prior to fulfilling mitzvot, we light the Shabbat candles before reciting the blessing. Why? Once we recite the blessing, we have welcomed in the Sabbath and at that point lighting would not generally be permissible. This is also the reason the eyes are covered; we don't want to see the light until after we make the blessing.

- Step One: Light the Candles.
- Step Two: Extend your hands towards the candles and with your palm facing your face, make a circular motion towards yourself three times then cover your eyes.
- Step Three: Recite the Blessing (below), and add appropriate prayers, if you wish.

The following blessing is recited after lighting the candles:
Blessed are You, Ado-noy, our God, King of the Universe, Who has made us holy with His commandments, and commanded us to light the Shabbat candles. All the Shabbat blessings are reproduced in English, Hebrew and are transliterated in Chapter 9.

Watch a video demonstration of 'Lighting Shabbat Candles', at SimplyJewishOnline.com/videodemonstrations.

Understanding Candle Lighting

If Shabbat is holy, then the Shabbat candle lighting is the Holy of Holies. The candle lighting marks the moment in time when we switch from our mundane weekday lives to the spiritual Shabbat. This is done with candles because the soul is compared to a candle, and the objective, as Friday night turns into Shabbat, is to kindle that soul. Two candles are used to symbolize that we have an 'extra soul' on the Shabbat, and also to recall the "remember" and "keep" the Sabbath language used in the ten Commandments.

Although the lighting may be done by anyone, it is typically reserved for the 'woman of the house'. Candle lighting is an effective time for prayer and many a woman uses this opportunity to pray for 'extra light' for the 'candles' (souls) in her family. The circular motions are done to show acceptance of Shabbat, to 'wave it in'.

Shalom Alaychem

After Shabbat has been welcomed with the candle lighting, and those who have prayed have returned from synagogue, we are ready to start the Shabbat meal.

The universally accepted custom is to start the meal by singing 'Shalom Alaychem'. Shalom Alaychem, literally meaning "peace be upon you", is still a commonly used greeting when Jews meet. The Shalom Alaychem song attempts to accomplish the same thing, welcoming all to the Shabbat table, including the heavenly angels that visit us every Friday night, (see Talmud, Tractate Shabbat 119:b).

> SINGING AYSHET CHAYIL TO THE 'WOMAN OF THE HOUSE' AS A (SMALL) TOKEN OF APPRECIATION...

The prevalent custom is to sing the four stanzas three times each, (some only recite each stanza one time). Please note that all the Shabbat blessings are reproduced in English, Hebrew and are transliterated in Chapter 9.

Ayshet Chayil (Woman of Valor)

A common, but not universal custom is to follow 'Shalom Alaychem' with another song, 'Ayshet Chayil'. Ayshet Chayil, or 'Woman of Valor' is a twenty-two verse poem attributed to King Solomon. The final chapter of Proverbs, it is an "ode to Jewish womanhood". Although most commentators interpret the poem allegorically, it has become the custom to sing Ayshet Chayil to the 'woman of the house' as a (small) token of appreciation for all she has done for the family. Ayshet Chayil is reproduced in English, Hebrew and transliterated in Chapter 9.

Blessing the Children

Next comes the blessing of the children. Each child is blessed individually. The father rests his hand on the child's head and bestows the blessing. The blessing given here, is merely the minimum. Adding specific, customized blessings for your child is appropriate. In many households, the children proceed to their mother to receive her blessing as well.

The first part of the blessing is different for a daughter and a son. The rest of the blessing is the same for both daughters and sons.

The blessing for a daughter:
May God make you like Sara, Rebecca, Rachel and Leah.

The blessing for a son:
May God make you like Ephraim and Menashe.
Conclude for both daughters and sons:
May God bless you and protect you.
May God shine His face towards you and show you favor.
May God be favorably disposed towards you and grant you peace.

The full text for the Blessings is reproduced in English, Hebrew and transliterated in Chapter 9.

Understanding "Blessing the Children"

What is more dear to us than our children? Nothing. Our children intuitively know this is true. Yet, during the hectic week, our actions may suggest otherwise. This one moment on a Friday night - as you place your hand on your son or daughter's head and lovingly bestow a heartfelt blessing - has the power to undo a full week of meetings and late nights spent working.

What is the source of the blessings? The second part of the blessing that is stated for both sons and daughters is taken directly from the Torah/Bible (Numbers 6:24); it is the "Priestly Blessing" that the priests bestowed upon the people of Israel.

The blessing for daughters is hardly a mystery. Blessing your daughter that she should be like the matriarchs is a powerful blessing. But why do we bless our sons to be like Ephraim and Menashe? Who were they anyway? Ephraim and Menashe were the sons of Joseph and the grandsons of the patriarch Jacob, and they were very righteous individuals. But why should they be the role models that our generation should aspire to? Wouldn't it be better to be like Abraham, Isaac, and Jacob – our patriarchs, or like Moses or King David?

Ephraim and Menashe were selected because they were born in Egypt. They were the first Jews born in exile. One stayed at home and studied

Torah with Grandfather Jacob and one became an important minister in Pharaoh's court; but they both remained steadfast in their belief. Today, with so many of our children seeking to make it in Pharaoh's court or its modern day equivalent, could there be a better role model? Using Ephraim and Menashe for role models says it is ok to want to be successful in the secular world, and that does not have to be at the expense of your Jewish beliefs.

Kiddush

© Hazorfim Ltd

Before discussing how to say Kiddush, let's look at what Kiddush is and why we would even want to say it. Kiddush means "make holy". God made the Sabbath (Shabbat) holy. We commemorate this by sanctifying the Shabbat over a goblet of wine. The moment of making Kiddush, (or listening to it) is one of great spiritual potential, as if the heavens are completely opened before you without any barriers. Kiddush is considered "testimony", as if we are "testifying" to our belief in God's creation of the world, and indeed, our very belief in God Himself.

How to Say Kiddush

Fill your wine goblet to the very top. While standing, hold the goblet in your primary hand and while standing recite the following:

It was evening, then morning of the sixth day and the Heaven and earth were completed, and all their hosts. And on the seventh day God completed the work He had been doing. And God blessed the seventh day and made it holy because on it God ceased His work of creating. Blessed are You, Ado-noy, our God, King of the Universe, Creator of the fruit of the vine.

Blessed are You, Ado-noy, our God, King of the Universe, Who made us holy with His commandments and favored us by giving us His holy Sabbath with love and favor as our heritage as a reminder of creation. It is the foremost day of the holy days marking the Exodus from Egypt. Because of all the nations, You chose us and made us holy and You gave us Your holy Sabbath out of love and favor, as our heritage. Blessed are You God, Who sanctifies the Shabbat.

The Hebrew and transliterated versions of Kiddush are reproduced in Chapter 9.

Kiddush "Insider"

Here are a few logistical points:

Kiddush is recited standing, although some have the custom to sit. The goblet is filled to the top. It is preferable to use a goblet, but any glass or cup that contains at least 4.2 ounces of wine is sufficient. Any kosher wine or grape juice may be used. Those present fulfill the mitzvah of Kiddush by listening and answering "Amen".

The person who made the blessing should not just drink from the goblet and then pass his goblet to other people. (Although you will fulfill the mitzvah, you will also 'gross out' your guests.) The preferred way is for the person who recited Kiddush to pour some wine from the goblet for himself (at least 2.1 ounces), and then pour from the goblet to the glasses of all those present.

Why do we fill the goblet to the top? The cup of wine is a cup of blessing and we want all the blessings in our life to be filled to the top. During Kiddush the challah is covered with a challah cover. Why? During the week, the blessing for bread precedes the blessing for wine. On the Sabbath, during the Kiddush the blessing over the wine precedes the blessing over the bread/challah. We cover the challah to avoid insulting it. You may think, bread is an inanimate object, how could it be offended? That is exactly the point. If we have to be sensitive to the challah, which won't be offended, how sensitive must we be to other people, who may be offended by our actions.

How to Wash for the Challah (Bread)

At the kitchen sink, an oversized cup is filled to the rim with water. Rings that one removes while washing or working should be taken off before this washing, so that the water can reach the entire hand. Holding the cup in your left hand, pour half its contents over your right hand, on both the inside and outside of the hand, up to the wrist, so that every part of your hand is wet. This should be done twice on the right hand, then twice on the left hand.

Before drying your hands, recite the following blessing:
Blessed are You, Ado-noy, our God, King of the Universe, Who has made us holy with His commandments, and commanded us regarding washing hands.

The full text for the Blessings is reproduced in English, Hebrew and transliterated in Chapter 9.

Watch a brief video demonstration of 'Washing for Bread/Challah', at SimplyJewishOnline.com/videodemonstrations.

Washing "Insider"

Here are a few logistical points regarding washing for challah. "My hands are not dirty, do I need to wash again"? Yes, wash again. This washing is more of a spiritual washing than a cleanliness washing. Many people purchase ornate washing cups to show their love for performing the mitzvot, but in truth, any large cup that holds at least 5 ounces is sufficient.
Again, the cup should be filled to the top, symbolizing our desire for God to fill us with material blessings.

Finally, from the time you wash your hands until you hear (or make) the blessing on the challah, you should not talk. The washing is integrally related to the blessing on the challah and talking would sever that connection.

Hamotzee: The Blessing on Challah

There are two challahs at every Shabbat meal. After everyone has returned to the table, pick up both challahs and recite the following blessing: *Blessed are You, Ado-noy, our God, King of the Universe, Who brings forth bread from the earth.*

The full text for the Blessing on Challah is reproduced in English, Hebrew and transliterated in Chapter 9.

After saying the blessing, cut the challah for all those present. Dip the challah into salt or sprinkle salt on the challah, and then pass it to everyone. After eating a piece of challah, normal conversation resumes.

Hamotzee "Insider"

This same blessing, "Hamotzee", is the blessing recited on all breads during the week. Bread, such an important staple, has always symbolized sustenance. The sages say that making this blessing with proper devotion is deemed as a source to merit sustenance, as it demonstrates your faith in the One that really brings forth the bread.

Why are there two challahs? After the Jewish people left Egypt (Passover), we sojourned in the desert for 40 years. During this time we were fed directly by God. A daily portion of manna fell six days a week, one portion for every person. Nothing fell on the Sabbath. Instead, on Fridays two portions fell, one for Friday and one for the Sabbath. It is to commemorate this event that we have two challahs at our Shabbat meal.

What's the deal with the salt? In the days of the holy Temple in Jerusalem, the altar offerings were salted. To commemorate this, at our table, which the Talmud likens to the altar, we symbolically (lightly) salt the challah.

Fresh Hot Challah

It is perfectly acceptable to purchase challahs (the actual plural is "challot".) Still, it must be acknowledged that there are few things in this world that can rival the taste of a warm challah.

I offer two suggestions. One is to take your store or bakery-purchased challah and wrap it in aluminum foil and right before candle lighting put it into your still warm (but turned off) oven.
The other idea is to do it the old fashioned way. Consider baking your own challah. Towards that end I have included the challah recipe of Jamie Geller, best selling author of *Quick & Kosher: Recipes From The Bride Who Knew Nothing*, (Chapter 9), with her gracious consent.

The Festive Shabbat Meal

In 'real time', the previous steps, from Shalom Alaychem through eating the challah, take only a few minutes, but their descriptions have taken a number of pages. The Shabbat meal is the exact opposite. Our description will be brief, but a festive meal with family and friends should not be.

Traditional fare is chicken soup, gefilte fish, chicken, potato kugel, and various salads, topped off with a crowd-pleasing dessert.

I again refer you to Jamie Geller and Resource VIII for recipes for chicken soup, chulent, and links to classic recipes and videos. The traditional fare is not etched in stone. There is no reason to force yourself to eat gefilte fish it if you dislike it. One of my students in Arizona commented that he wasn't really loving the chicken soup after walking home from services on a day that the temperature reached 107 degrees. You can certainly pass on the soup. Indeed, you can modify any facet of the menu to meet the your needs and the needs of your guests. The main objective is to have a good, tasty, kosher meal that you and your guests will enjoy.

Zmeerot – Singing at the Shabbat Table

One of the more enjoyable ways in which a Shabbat meal differs from a weekday meal is the singing of Zmeerot (songs). The traditional songs are found in a 'bentcher', (so-called because their main purpose is that they contain the 'bentching', the Birkat Hamazon or grace after meals). We use the NCSY Bentcher, because it has the words in Hebrew, English, and is transliterated. If your family is very musical you will enjoy this family sing-a-long very much. If your family is 'musically challenged', don't worry. This custom is an enhancer of the Sabbath, and not a rigid requirement of it.

The D'var Torah-Sharing Words of Torah

Another way the Shabbat meal is enhanced is through sharing words of Torah. Although it's not formally required, the importance of saying some words of Jewish wisdom can't be overstated. Why? Sharing these words of Jewish wisdom spiritually elevates the entire meal. First of all, Shabbat meals should not be reduced exclusively to discussions about sports, politics and the latest movies. Whenever Jews get together and break bread, certainly on the Holy Shabbat, the meal should have a spiritual component as well. Even more importantly, sharing words of Torah demonstrates to our children, the next generation of Jews, what our core values are.

Does this mean making some type of speech? Not necessarily. The 'D'var Torah' does not have to be formal or lengthy. I personally like a discussion better than a speech format, but it is a matter of style. Potential topics abound. They include a question or point of interest from the weekly Torah reading; or the approaching Jewish holiday, (there is always an approaching holiday); a story that has a good moral lesson, or a current event that has an appropriate lesson. Recently, while entertaining a big sports fan, we explored baseball players who are asked to testify against their friends from the perspective of Jewish law. Another week we discussed whether the Jewish law requiring one to recite a blessing upon seeing a king, applies to the President of the United States. Another week, close to Passover, we discussed what qualities Moses possessed that led God to select him as the leader of the Jewish People (and what it means to us today). There is literally a world of possibilities.

Grace-After-Meals; Birkat Hamazon or Bentching

The Grace-After-Meals is either sung together or recited quietly at the table at the conclusion of the meal. Some families sing the first paragraph together and then each person completes the prayer on their own. The entire Grace-After-Meals is reproduced in Chapter 9 in Hebrew, English and phonetically.

Grace-After-Meals "Insider"

The 'Grace-After-Meals' is the only blessing explicitly mentioned in the Torah. Why is it so important? After enjoying God's bounty, we should acknowledge and thank Him for it. Does God really need to hear us thank Him? (For that matter, does God need to hear us pray?) No, God is omnipotent and just fine whether we thank Him or not. We need to thank Him for our own sakes. By thanking those who help us, we become better, more appreciative people, and this is a lesson taught to us by God Himself.

In much of the world (excluding Israel), you may hear 'Grace-After-Meals' referred to as 'bentching', a shortened (Yiddish) version of the words meaning 'blessing'. In Israel people refer to 'Grace-After-Meals' as 'Birkat Hamazon', the Hebrew term, and they don't generally use the term 'bentching'.

Shabbat Morning

Shabbat morning, after services, the second Shabbat meal takes place. Like Friday night, it is preceded by Kiddush, washing for Challah, and making the Hamotzee blessing on the Challah. The Shabbat day meal is typically a bit less 'grand' than the Friday night meal. Nonetheless, it is a festive, family-oriented meal, and it is appropriate to have good food, complete with 'Zmeerot' and 'words of Torah'. A popular dish during the Shabbat day meal is 'chulent', a stew of meat, potatoes, barley, lentils and various other ingredients. It is left cooking from before the Sabbath, as a means of having a hot meal during the time when cooking is prohibited. (For a 'chulent' recipe from Jamie Geller, see Chapter 9). The text of the Shabbat morning Kiddush is different from Friday night. It is reproduced in Chapter 9.

Havdalah: Shabbat's Closing Ceremony

This ceremony consists of blessings that are recited over wine (or grape juice), spices and a special candle.

First, fill your cup of wine to the rim and beyond, until it flows over the rim, as this is a cup of blessing and we want all our blessings to overflow. Then light the special havdalah candle. The 'Hamavdil' blessing is recited. Those present say 'Amen' and at least a half of the wine is drunk by the person who recited the blessing. The full text of Havdalah is reproduced in Chapter 9.

Havdalah "Insider"

Havdalah is the ceremony during which we end Shabbat. Just as we 'bring in' Shabbat with honor, we escort it out with honor as well.

When is Shabbat over? The Talmud tells us that Shabbat ends when we can see "three medium sized stars". For all us city slickers, an easier way to calculate the end of the Shabbat anywhere in the United States (except Alaska and the presently uninhabited area north west of Madawaska Maine), is by adding one hour and six minutes to the time the sun has set, (sunset is listed in every newspaper). Many Jews exercise the optional, though meritorious custom of extending the Shabbat.

What spices may be used? Cloves are the most common, but any pleasant smelling spice may be used. The purpose of the spice is to 'comfort our souls' because we believe that when the Shabbat departs, along with it goes a part of our souls, (we have an 'extra soul', or component of our soul on Shabbat).

The Havdalah Candle. This blessing is recited to commemorate Adam's first fire on the first Saturday night of creation. The Havdalah candle is a special wax candle with multiple wicks. We start Shabbat lighting single wick candles. We end it by lighting this multiple wick candle. Our soul is represented by a candle. It is our hope that our 'candle' has grown during the Shabbat.

Making the Shabbat Holy

A number of years ago, when I was in college, I spent Shabbat with some friends in their dormitory apartment. Shabbat candles were lit. Kiddush was recited. All the steps described in this book were performed. The friends also had another interesting custom; they left on their television. Throughout the Shabbat meal, people were shuttling back and forth to check on a hockey game. Now, they did not technically 'violate' the Sabbath, but nor did they 'make it Holy'. It was certainly not a very spiritually uplifting Shabbat meal.

Shabbat is like most things in life. You get out of it what you invest in it. If you treat Shabbat like an ordinary day, then that is exactly what it will be. But if you treat it like a special day, then that is exactly what it will be.

CHAPTER THREE:
Major Holidays

The Jewish calendar features both major and minor holidays. Very similar to the lifecycle events, our calendar commemorates days that are joyous and days that are sorrowful. This chapter focuses on the major holidays; the next chapter focuses on lesser holidays, fast days, and days of remembrance.

PASSOVER

Passover is the holiday that commemorates the 'Exodus' of the Jewish People from slavery in Egypt. The "Seder", the meal at which we recount the story of Passover, is by far the most observed ritual of the Jewish calendar.

The Passover Story

In response to one of the worst famines in the history of the world, Jacob and his seventy descendants accepted an invitation to sojourn to Egypt. As time passed, the Jewish People became more numerous and more prosperous, causing envy among the local populace (sound familiar?). The Jews were too powerful, yet too valuable to simply expel. Instead, the Jews were enslaved.

What does slavery mean? It is a difficult concept for our generation to grasp. If you hear the term at all, it is likely pertaining to things like too much homework, or one extra workplace or household chore. (Indeed, it is in reference to Passover cleaning that I have heard it most.) Slavery really means that you are under the complete control and domination of another human being 24/7. For starters, to get a more accurate picture of slavery, I recommend reading descriptions by Holocaust survivors of what it really meant to be a slave. (Elie Weisel's *Night*, is a good example).

The Jews were slaves in Egypt for 210 years. Egypt was the reigning superpower. No person had ever escaped its borders. The slavery was especially brutal, designed to break the body and spirit. It wasn't enough to build buildings (pyramids?) in the hot sun under a taskmaster's whip. The buildings were intentionally built in quicksand, to prolong the project, and to assure there would never be the satisfaction of accomplishment. If the daily quota of mortar was not achieved, the amount was supplemented by adding Jewish babies. When Pharaoh heard that a Jewish savior would be born, he ordered that all baby boys be put to death.

Amidst this gloom, God did save His People. First God selected Moses as their leader. Ironically, Moses was raised as a prince in Pharaoh's own palace. God liberated the Jewish People with a 'mighty arm', devastating the Egyptians with the Ten Plagues that were quite literally of Biblical proportions.

The plagues initially struck the Egyptian gods (for example, since the Egyptians worshipped the Nile, its water turned to blood), but soon devastated their possessions and ultimately their bodies. After the last plague, the death of the firstborn, the Egyptians urged the Jews to leave

immediately. The Jews did not even have enough time to fully bake their bread. Instead, they took the bread before it rose and it looked like a matzah. To commemorate this, we are given the mitzvah to eat matzah; (Deuteronomy 16:1-8). The Torah also prohibits eating chametz, (or even owning chametz), during the entire Passover holiday; (Deuteronomy 16:3-4). "Chametz" is the term for leavened products such as bread, cereal, cake and pasta.

The Fast of the Firstborn

To commemorate the final plague in which God killed the firstborn Egyptians and "passed over" the Jewish houses, Jewish firstborns fast the day before Passover.

If people want to fast they may certainly do so; however, that is not the common practice. Since this fast is not considered an obligatory fast, compared to the obligatory Day of Atonement/Yom Kippur fast, firstborns instead attend a special festive celebration in which a Talmudic tractate is completed. Participation in the festive completion of the tractate supersedes this fast, and one is permitted to eat.

How to Make a Seder

A lot of people look forward to the four cups of wine. Others anxiously await the first taste of matzah. As important as the wine and matzah are, the single most important facet of the Seder is the recounting of the Exodus story to our children. It is how we became a nation, and how we remain a nation.

The Seder is meant to be more than a ritual; it is meant to be a way for us to transmit to our children our belief and our heritage. While the Seder is an appropriate time to have company, it should not be at the expense of your children. The emphasis on children is apparent throughout the Seder. It is why the children ask the 'four questions', hide the afikomen, and so on. At my family Seder we go even further. We have visual aids for the ten plagues (red powder in water to make it look like blood, jumping frogs, etc.); we act out a few short skits, such as Pharaoh telling the midwives to kill the Jewish baby boys, Moses being placed in a basket in the Nile; (for some reason, I am always cast as Pharaoh.)

Things You Will Need In Advance

1. A Haggadah. The special prayer book for the Seder contains far more than the prayers. It compiles the verses, sayings, stories, commentaries, and songs in the traditional order. (The word 'Seder' actually means 'order'). I personally recommend the

ArtScroll Haggadah, or The *ArtScroll Children's Haggadah*, because the English translation is very good, but there are literally dozens of haggadahs to choose from.

2. Wine or grape juice (enough for four cups).
3. Matzah. (at least three unbroken matzahs and enough for all participants to have an ample amount).
4. A Matzah cover.
5. A Seder plate, the large ornamental plate that has places designated for all the required items. Making one with your children in advance is an economical alternative that will help set the tone for the holiday.

Items Needed for the Seder Plate and at the Seder

Prior to the start of the holiday make sure you have the following items that you will need for the seder plate.

1. Karpas: A vegetable, such as celery or boiled potato.
2. Chazeret and Maror: Romaine lettuce and horseradish.
3. Baytzah: One roasted egg.
4. Charoset: A mix of wine, nuts, apple, and cinnamon.
5. Zeroah: One roasted (shank) bone.
6. Salt water.
7. 'Elijah's Cup' - one extra wine goblet for Elijah the Prophet, who according to tradition visits every Seder.
8. A pillow - Although a pillow is not a requirement per se, it will aid in the required 'reclining'. To celebrate our freedom we recline like royalty, leaning to our left side at certain key points of the seder, such as when we eat the matzah and drink the four cups of wine

9. A small 'Afikomen' bag or large napkin. The Afikomen is part of the matzah broken off and put into the bag (explained below).

Understanding the Seder Plate

As mentioned earlier, the Seder plate has six designated places; let's explain what each one is and what it represents.

1. Karpas. This vegetable, historically a green one, is meant to symbolize rebirth and spring (another name for Passover is 'holiday of the spring').
2. Marror. The bitter herbs symbolize the bitter treatment of the Jewish slaves.
3. Baytzah. The roasted egg is a reminder of the festival offering brought in the Temple.

4. Charoset. This mixture of wine, apples, nuts and cinnamon is a symbol of the mortar (for bricks) made by the slaves.
5. Zeroah. The roasted (shank) bone is a symbol of the Pascal lamb offered in the Temple on Passover eve.
6. Salt Water. This is a reminder of the bitter tears shed by our ancestors, the slaves.

The Seder

With your Haggadah in hand follow the 'order' of the Seder:

1. Kadesh. We recite Kiddush over wine as we do every Shabbat and holiday. This is the 1st of the four cups of wine.
2. Ur'chatz. We wash our hands without reciting the customary blessing. This is done to arouse the curiosity of the children.
3. Karpas. We dip the vegetables in salt water. This is also done to arouse the curiosity of the children.
4. Yachatz. The 'leader' breaks the middle matzah and hides the Afikomen.
5. Maggid. We tell the Passover story through reading the Haggadah. You may supplement the reading with whatever visual aide you deem appropriate.
6. Rachtza. We wash our hands before having matzah, this time saying the customary blessing (al netilat yadayeam).

7. Motzi. We recite the Hamotzee blessing over the matzah.
8. Matzah. We recite the special blessing for eating the matzah; then we eat the matzah.
9. Marror. We recite the special blessing and eat the bitter herb.
10. Koraych. We eat a sandwich of bitter herbs inside matzah.
11. Shulchan Orech. We enjoy the festive meal.
12. Tzafoon. We eat the afikomen.
13. Baraych. We recite the Birkat Hamazon, 'grace-after-meals'.
14. Hallel. We recite (or sing) Hallel.
15. Neartzah. We sing additional songs, concluding the Seder with 'chad gadya' and wishing that "next year we should be in Jerusalem".

'Taking' the Afikomen

If you're a child, this is one of the highlights of your Seder. The leader of the Seder, let's call him Grandpa (but it can be anyone), breaks off part of the middle Matzah, ('Yachatz'), and places it into a small matzah bag. Any type of bag will do, but one made by your child as an arts and crafts project is especially appropriate. Grandpa leaves the bag in Junior's line of vision and then a few minutes later conveniently turns his attention elsewhere. At this point, Junior swipes the afikomen and hides it. Grandpa eventually notices it's missing and then searches for the lost afikomen, but not too strenuously. Since the afikomen is required for the latter stages of the Seder, Grandpa must provide some type of (minor) 'incentive' to Junior to facilitate its return.

Are we training our children to be thieves and extortionists? Hardly. It's just another way of involving the children by making the Seder fun for them.

ROSH HASHANAH

Typically coinciding with the end of summer vacation, is the approach of "the High Holidays." Rosh Hashanah and Yom Kippur are collectively referred to as "the High Holidays".

Rosh Hashanah is the Jewish New Year, (literally the 'head of the year'). It is the anniversary of God's creation of mankind and the day that God sits in judgment of all creation. Rosh Hashanah is the day the 'Shofar', (ram's horn) is sounded 100 times during services. The Shofar is not intended to demonstrate an ancient musical instrument, nor is it meant to be an empty ritual. It is meant to be a 'wake up call', to rouse us out of our spiritual slumber.

How to 'Do' Rosh Hashanah

The mitzvah of the day is to hear the Shofar. Still, if you went to hear the Shofar and listened to it very carefully and did nothing else, you would have missed the point of Rosh Hashanah. Rosh Hashanah is a time to 'take stock', to measure where you are in your relationships with God and man.

Another ritual performed on Rosh Hashanah is 'Tashlich'. We walk to the nearest river, brook, or stream, recite a special prayer and 'throw our sins away'. Alas, if only it was so simple. This is only symbolic. If you have done something wrong you must still make amends.

The Rosh Hashanah prayers are recited from a special prayer book called a 'Machzor'. The prayers and services are lengthier than during the rest of the year, and now that we have English translations and understand what we are saying, we see that some of the High Holiday prayers are actually a little scary.

What are we supposed to think? That God is 'out to get us' and give us a bad year (or worse), unless we spend the day groveling and begging? Does God love us? Yes, God, our Father in heaven, loves us very much, more than we can possibly realize. Surprised? For some reason this fact is not well publicized today, but it has always been so.

If God loves us so much, why does He judge us on Rosh Hashanah? Because not judging us would mean that there would be no consequences to our actions, and no significance to our choices and struggles, and that would surely not be love. To understand the idea more fully we must ask ourselves the timeless question, "Why am I here"?

If you think you are here in this world primarily just to physically live life to its fullest, then a Day of Judgment is very troubling. If you think you are here to live life to its fullest including growing spiritually and accomplishing it in ways that will reflect well upon you at the end of your life, then an annual review, while not always comfortable, is very important.

YOM KIPPUR

The tenth day after the Day of Judgment is the Day of Atonement, the holiest day of the year.

Yom Kippur is the Day of Atonement. It is the great day that God gives us to atone for our sins. Contrary to popular perception, God is not looking for perfection; He created us and knows that perfection is not possible. He is however, looking for growth and a sincere attempt at improvement. The fast is meant to remind us of our angel-like qualities and is not meant to be punitive.

How to 'Do' Yom Kippur

Many people define Yom Kippur by the mandatory fast. Although the fast is important, the key to the day is to utilize the opportunity to seek atonement and repent for our sins and indiscretions. Seeking atonement from God is relatively easy. After all, God is our father and wants to forgive us. Seeking atonement from other people is often more difficult. Nonetheless, we are required to seek forgiveness when we have wronged others. If someone sincerely seeks forgiveness, we are encouraged to accept it graciously.

Repentance in Judaism is not merely 'lip service'. Sincere repentance includes remorse and the resolution to never do the inappropriate act again.

How should the day be spent? Someone who takes a heavy dose sleeping pill and sleeps the day away has not violated the fast but has completely missed the point of the day. Besides fasting and praying, the day really should be spent reflecting and resolving; reflecting on your life and goals and resolving what you can realistically and specifically do better. The bad news is that just resolving to 'do better' is so non-specific and open ended as to render it virtually meaningless. The good news is that no one is expected to change overnight. Picking one specific thing and sticking to it is very powerful.

Some examples from a recent study group included, "Say the (one minute long) Shemah Yisrael prayer daily", "Talk more pleasantly to a co-worker who makes me crazy", "Light Shabbat candles every Friday night", "Not to beep my horn at other drivers until I count to ten", and "Attend a weekly Torah class." If you work on one item a year every year you will grow tremendously.

In addition to fasting, other prohibitions on Yom Kippur include drinking, washing, anointing, wearing leather shoes, and marital relations.

SUKKOT

After the serious High Holidays, we change gears, entering into a more festive holiday period. Sukkot is a seven day Biblical festival celebrated by eating in the Sukkah (a temporary outdoor hut). It commemorates our 40 year existence in the desert, after leaving Egypt on the way to Israel.

How to 'Do' Sukkot

To properly celebrate Sukkot you will need a Sukkah and "the four species".

Sukkot come in many different sizes and styles including the 'make it yourself variety'. Building and then decorating a Sukkah is a great family bonding experience. The basic requirements are rather straightforward:

1. Generally, three walls are required (4 walls are better).
2. The walls can be made of any material. Using the side of your house is allowed.
3. The walls must be made before the roof is put on.
4. The walls must be strong enough to withstand an 'ordinary wind'.
5. The roof must be made of 'natural' material, such as branches or cornhusks.

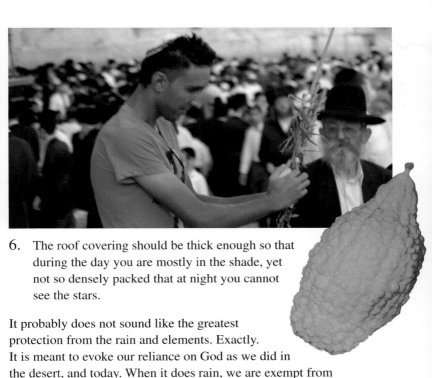

6. The roof covering should be thick enough so that during the day you are mostly in the shade, yet not so densely packed that at night you cannot see the stars.

It probably does not sound like the greatest protection from the rain and elements. Exactly. It is meant to evoke our reliance on God as we did in the desert, and today. When it does rain, we are exempt from the mitzvah of Sukkah.

Sukkot is also celebrated by reciting a blessing upon the "four species". The four include the lulav (a palm branch), etrog (a citron), hadassim (myrtle branches), and aravot (willows). The blessing is recited on the lulav each day of Sukkot except Shabbat. Although people commonly refer to "taking the lulav", the blessing is only recited if all four of the species are present and intact.

The blessing for eating in the Sukkah and the blessing for taking the Lulav are reproduced in Chapter 9.

SHMINI ATZERET AND SIMCHAT TORAH

The holidays of Shmini Atzeret and Simchat Torah are celebrated after Sukkot. In Israel they are celebrated on the same day, and in the rest of the Jewish world they are celebrated on consecutive days. Shmini Atzeret, the eighth day from the start of Sukkot, is an "added day". It is a day really devoid of any special mitzvot, a day given to us to symbolically demonstrate God's wish to extend our visit with Him for one additional day.

Simchat Torah is literally translated as the "Joy of Torah". It marks our completion of the weekly Torah reading cycle. In many observant communities, it is celebrated with great joy and fervor as befits a day that honors our most important legacy. Typically, all the Torah scrolls are taken from the Ark for seven joyous trips (Hakafot) around the synagogue. As the Torah passes by, it is customary to kiss the Torah, showing our love for it. It is considered a great honor to be called to the Torah for the last 'aliyah' of the Torah. Once we complete the Torah, we immediately start from Genesis, symbolizing that we are never really finished with the Torah.

CHANUKAH

Two full months pass between the end of Simchat Torah and the next holiday, Chanukah.

Chanukah, second only to Passover in its ritual observance, is probably our most misunderstood holiday.

Most people's knowledge of Chanukah is limited to knowing that we light the menorah (but they don't know why we do so), and that there are "eight crazy nights". Let's see if we can do a little better. Chanukah, "the festival of lights", is observed by lighting candles in a menorah, (technically a 'chanukiyah'), in ascending order during each of its eight nights. On the first night we light one candle, and on the eighth night we light eight. Why do we light the menorah? The menorah was lit daily in the Temple and only pure oil was used. At that time in history, the Greeks controlled the Temple. When the Jews, loyal to the Torah, recaptured the Temple, they saw that it was desecrated with idols and they could not locate any pure oil to light the menorah. No oil, that is, except one container, enough to last one day. The process of replacing the oil with new oil took eight days. Miraculously, the one container of oil lasted eight days, until the new supply arrived.

In truth, Chanukah was really about the loyal, taxpaying Jewish subjects, rebelling against the mighty Syrian/Greek Empire when it attempted to ban the practice of our religion. During its first 2,100 years, the holiday was celebrated by lighting the menorah and giving children sweets and a few coins to play dreidel. The greatest irony is that the holiday that commemorated Jews who stood up to the dominant culture, has been so radically changed due to its tendency to occur in late December, close to a certain other holiday celebrated by the dominant culture.

The Jews loyal to our faith were led by the "Maccabees". Initially, they were just one family, patriarch Mattisyahu and his five sons, Judah, Jonathon, Shimon, Elazar, and Yochanan. It would be fair to observe that one person can make a difference. At first the Maccabees were just a small group hiding in the Judean mountains launching nocturnal raids on modest targets. Eventually, they grew in strength and boldness and with God's help, not only stood toe to toe with a world power, but defeated it, despite the great numeric superiority of the enemy.

How to Light

Each night, before lighting the Chanukah candles, you light an additional candle called the 'Shamash'. The actual Chanukah candles are lit with the Shamash. On the first night you light one candle. The candle is the one furthest to the right as you look out the window, (and furthest to the left if you were outside the window looking in). On the second night you add a second candle. You light the second candle first, followed by the candle you lit the first night. Follow the same procedure every night.

After lighting the Shamash, but prior to lighting the Chanukah candles, two blessings are recited. On the first night, however, a third blessing is added. After lighting the candles, it is customary to sing "Rock of Ages/Maoz Tzur". The blessings and "Rock of Ages" are reproduced in Chapter 9.

When to Light

The candles may be lit from the time it gets dark outside until there are people awake to see the lit menorah (either outside or inside). The ideal time to light is the first minute you are allowed to because this demonstrates our love for doing mitzvot. However, waiting for a family member to return home and participate in this joyous mitzvah, trumps doing it at the earliest time. On Friday night the candles are lit much earlier, before the Shabbat candles, because lighting on Shabbat is not permitted. Ordinarily, a candle that lasts 30 minutes is sufficient. On Friday nights longer lasting candles are required, so that they burn until 30 minutes after the stars come out, a total of about 120 minutes., (in the United States, excluding Alaska).

Where to Light

The reason we light the Chanukah menorah is to commemorate and publicize the miracle of the oil that lasted for eight days. Since we are bid to publicize the miracle, the best places to light are the places where people will see the candles; in front of a window that faces the street, or in the doorway to your home. In Israel many people actually light outside.

How to Play Dreidel

One of the ways to make Chanukah fun for children is to "play dreidel". A dreidel is like a four-sided top. On each side is a Hebrew letter. On one side is a "nun", standing for "nais" or "miracle". If you land on the "nun", you neither win nor lose. On the second side is a "gimel", standing for "gadol" or "big". If you land on "gimel", you are the big winner and you take whatever is in the pot. On the third side is the letter "Hey", standing for "hahya" or "happened". If you land on "hey", you get half the pot. (Hey, that's better than nothing) On the last side is the letter "shin", standing for "sham" or "there". If you land on "shin", you must contribute to the pot. Put all the letters together and you have, "a great miracle happened there". In Israel the dreidel is a little different. The letter "shin" is replaced with the letter "pay" standing for "poe" or "here", because the miracle happened in Israel.

Everyone starts out with the same number of coins (or even better, chocolate coins), and at the start of the game and after the pot has been emptied, everyone must contribute to fund the pot. Everyone takes a turn spinning.

Here are a few more important points about Chanukah. Any type of menorah is permissible, as long as the candles are at the same height and in a line, (so people can easily tell how many candles are lit). Although just about any type of menorah and candles that can be lit may be used, and the colorful wax candles are perfectly acceptable (and pretty), the best way to fulfill the mitzvah is with an oil menorah, because that is how the menorah was lit in the Temple.

Electric menorahs may be used for ornamental purposes, but not for the actual lighting ceremony and blessings, because they are not "lit".

It is also customary to have some food that is prepared with oil on Chanukah. This is also done to commemorate the oil lasting eight days. Two favorites include "latkes" (fried potato pancakes), and jelly donuts.

PURIM

The longest stretch without a holiday culminates with Purim, probably the happiest day of the Jewish calendar.

The first Temple was destroyed in the year 422 BCE by Nevuchadnetzar and the Babylonians. The Babylonians were eventually replaced as the most dominant world power by the Persians. During his reign, King Achashverosh of Persia, at the urging of his anti-Semitic prime minister, Haman, signed a decree that authorized the murder of every Jewish man, woman, and child. Haman selected the date for the decree to be carried out, by using a lottery, or "pur" in Hebrew. He used many lotteries so the holiday is called Purim.

Queen Esther, whom the king didn't even know was Jewish, and Mordechai, the great sage, were able to reverse the decree, with God's unseen hand presiding over an amazing array of 'coincidences'. We understand Queen Esther's mission, to plead with the king to reverse the evil decree. But what role did Mordechai have? Actually, he had an even harder job. Mordechai had to convince all the Jews of different backgrounds that the true cause of the decree was not Haman. It was really due to Jews acting inappropriately, and that the salvation would be repentance and Jewish unity. Because Mordechai succeeded in his mission, Esther succeeded in hers.

Purim "Insider"

We celebrate the holiday by gathering and reading Megillat Esther, (the story of Purim from a hand-written parchment scroll), sending small presents of food to friends, giving charity, and enjoying a festive meal. Oh yes, and to commemorate how things are not quite how they appear on the surface, it is customary to wear a costume on Purim.

SHAVUOT

The third of the three Biblical festivals, Shavuot is the anniversary of the day that God gave us the Torah on Mount Sinai. It is odd that so many of our people are not even aware of the existence of this important holiday.

The name of the holiday, "Shavuot", or "weeks", commemorates the seven full weeks between Passover and receiving the Torah. At first blush this may seem like an odd name. What is being conveyed by calling the holiday "weeks" is the connecting of the Passover exodus to the receiving the Torah. Why? Because without receiving the Torah the Jews would have been no different than any other ancient people and the Jewish People and the Passover story would have been forgotten long ago. We are literally counting the weeks and the days in excitement until we receive the Torah.

The Torah reading recounts the giving of the Torah and includes the "Ten Commandments". If one were to examine the verses (Exodus 20:2), you would observe something very interesting. Unlike every other religion in which God speaks only to one person, God gave the Torah to the entire Jewish People. This is a critical difference. Practitioners of any other religion believe that just one person faithfully transmitted what God said to them. We believe that God spoke to our entire nation, publicly. Famously, Cecil B. Demille got it wrong in The Ten Commandments. God did not give the Torah to Moses privately. (I guess you should stick with the book and not the movie.)

Shavuot is sometimes jokingly referred to as 'the cheesecake holiday'. When the Torah was first given on that first Shavuot, we received the laws, including the ban on eating dairy and meat together. Since the nation did not have immediate access to additional sets of dishes, they used their dishes only for dairy. We commemorate this by eating dairy on Shavuot. Eating cheesecake is only a popular application of this concept. Certainly, eating less caloric, healthier, dairy dishes is perfectly acceptable.

The Book of Ruth is also read on Shavuot. One reason it is read is because Ruth is a story of a woman who sincerely converted to Judaism, taking upon herself all of the mitzvot, not just the 'cool ones', logical ones, or easy ones. The goal on Shavuot is to emulate Ruth and accept the Torah with the same level of commitment.

TISHA B'AV

During the summer, the calendar shifts to an annual mourning period, which culminates with the saddest day of the Jewish year.

On this, the saddest day of the Jewish year, we commemorate the loss of both Temples, as well as all the other tragedies that have occurred on this date, the 9th ('tisha') day of the Jewish month of Av.

On Tisha B'Av, eating and drinking, bathing, marital relations, and wearing leather shoes are all prohibited, as we are meant to feel like mourners. As important as the fasting and other restrictions are, the day should be a day of reflection and contemplation.

A student once asked, "The Temple was destroyed 2,000 years ago, why should we still mourn it"? The answer is that we are not merely mourning the loss of the building, but rather what it represents. If one of our major goals during our lifetime is to forge a relationship with God, then the loss of the Temple is a major setback, because the Temple afforded us the best opportunity to connect spiritually with God. Every tragedy that has befallen the Jewish People since the Temple was destroyed has had its origins in this loss.

The first Temple was destroyed by Nevuchadnetzar and the Babylonians in the year 422 BCE. The Second Temple was destroyed by the Romans in the year 69 A.D. Vespasian conquered much of Israel and surrounded Jerusalem, but when he was appointed as the new Caesar, he assigned his son Titus to finish the job. Titus did so with great cruelty. According to the historian Josephus, over one million Jews perished, a staggering number in the ancient world. The 'Arch of Titus' commemorates Titus' defeat of Israel and may still be seen in Rome today.

The Talmud tells us that the first Temple was destroyed because the Jews violated the three cardinal sins of murder, idol worship, and adultery. The first Temple was rebuilt after 70 years. The second Temple was destroyed because of 'baseless hatred', and has not been rebuilt for close to 2,000 years. Lest we point our fingers to the generation that experienced the destruction and think, "if only they could have gotten along a little better", the Talmud tells us that if the Temple was not rebuilt in your generation, it would have been destroyed in your generation.

So where does that leave us? Every time we argue, resent people, hold grudges, and certainly when we 'hate' wide swaths of people because we disagree with them, we are actually contributing to the problem. Conversely, each time we are like Aaron the High Priest, and "love peace and pursue peace", (Pirkay Avot 1:12), we are rebuilding the Temple, Jerusalem Stone by Jerusalem Stone.

CHAPTER FOUR:

Minor Holidays, Fast Days, & Days of Remembrance

TU B'SHVAT

What Is Tu B' Shvat?

Tu B'Shvat is called the New Year's Day for trees. It is considered the day that the produce of the land of Israel starts to ripen. It is a day to recall the goodness of the produce of the land of Israel. The name is derived from the date it occurs on the calendar, the fifteenth ("tu" stands for the Hebrew numbers that represent 15) day of the month of Shvat.

How Is It Observed?

On Tu B'Shvat it is customary to eat produce from the land of Israel, particularly the kind that the land of Israel is praised for, such as dates and figs, although other types are acceptable as well. Some have the custom of planting trees or paying for the planting of trees in Israel.

LAG B'OMER

What Is Lag B'Omer?

Lag B'Omer is the 33rd day of the omer ("lag" stands for the Hebrew numbers that represent 33). The omer is the 49 day period between the holidays of Passover and Shavuot. Although we are ultimately joyous as we get closer to the Shavuot holiday because it is the anniversary of our receiving the Torah, the early part of the omer is a time of mourning; therefore, weddings, haircuts and listening to live music are banned.

We mourn the untimely passing of 24,000 students of the great Rabbi Akiva during the Roman era. Lag B'Omer is the day the deaths suddenly ended. It is also the day of the passing of the great Rabbi Shimon Bar-Yochai. Typically, the day of passing of a great person would be a day of mourning. Rabbi Shimon's passing was different for two reasons. His death of natural causes consolidated his success in escaping the Roman execution decree against him. Additionally, Rabbi Shimon, a great Kabbalist, used the day of his passing as the time to teach his students many great kabbalistic secrets. These teachings were recorded in a book called "the Zohar" ("the light"). Thus, the secrets shared by Rabbi Shimon on the day of his passing transformed the day into a day of great joy.

How Is It Celebrated?

The bans in place during the mourning period come to an end on Lag B'Omer. Lag B'Omer is a very festive day, particularly in Israel and in the vicinity of Rabbi Shimon's burial place in Meron. The day is celebrated with dancing, singing, and bonfires. The bonfires are meant to allude to "the light", the book that recorded Rabbi Shimon's teachings. Children play with toy bows and arrows as a reminder that rainbows were never seen during Rabbi Shimon's lifetime.

Rainbows represent God's promise in Genesis 9:12-17 to never again destroy the world with a flood. Seeing a rainbow means that had God not given this promise, the world would be deserving of another flood. Rabbi Shimon's merit was so great, that during his lifetime, rainbows were never seen.

FAST DAYS

The Jewish calendar contains six fast days. We have already discussed the two most important ones, Yom Kippur and Tisha B'Av. In general, fast days are only applicable to those medically able to fast. The definition of "medically able to fast" is even less stringent during the four "minor" fasts.

Why Do We Fast?

Is the purpose forced dieting? Affliction? The major purpose of a fast day is to encourage us to take stock and assess our actions. The pangs of hunger go a long way towards helping people think. As noted earlier, someone who spends the day sleeping or working so busily that they do not have time to think, has missed the purpose of the fast day.

THE FAST OF GEDALYAH

When Is It?

The Fast of Gedalyah takes place on the third day of the Jewish year, the day after Rosh Hashanah.

What is the reason for this fast?

Gedalyah was the Jewish governor, appointed by the Babylonians after they destroyed the First Temple. Gedalyah was assassinated by fellow Jews jealous of his position. The Babylonians, who had been inclined to allow the small remnant of Jews live with a measure of autonomy, were unimpressed with this act of rebellion. They killed thousands of Jews, and many others fled to Egypt. The fast of Gedalyah marked the end of Jewish autonomy and demonstrates what happens when brother turns against brother.

THE FAST OF THE TENTH OF TEVET

When Is It?

The Fast of the Tenth of Tevet takes place on the tenth day of the Jewish month, Tevet (about a week after the end of Chanukah).

What Is the Reason for this Fast?

The fast commemorates the day that the Babylonians laid siege to Jerusalem, leading directly to the destruction of the First Temple.

THE FAST OF ESTHER

When Is It?

The Fast of Esther takes place on the day before Purim.

What is the Reason for this Fast?

As we related in more detail in the previous chapter, Purim is the most joyous of Jewish holidays, and Esther is the heroine of the day. Before she asked King Achashverosh to rescind the decree to kill all Jews, she first asked "the real king", God, for assistance. At Esther's request, all Jews fasted. We fast to commemorate their fast.

THE FAST OF THE 17TH OF TAMMUZ

When Is It?

The Fast of the 17th of Tammuz takes place on the 17th day of the Jewish month of Tammuz. (It typically occurs during July.)

What Is the Reason for this Fast?

The fast commemorates the day that the Romans breached Jerusalem's walls, leading directly to the destruction of the second Temple three weeks later. We know that the walled city of Jerusalem was very small by modern standards, and that it takes ten minutes to walk from the gates of the city to the Temple. We know that the Temple was not destroyed for another seven months. We can only imagine the intense suffering that occurred during these seven months and during the siege that preceded it. On this same date, Moses, upon witnessing the worship of the golden calf, broke the first set of the tablets that he received from God. Although only a small number of Jews were actually worshipping the idol, it was sinful for the masses to be neutral.

OTHER DAYS OF REMEMBRANCE

During the past seventy years, the Jewish people have experienced some of the most unbelievable events, both good and bad, and days of remembrance have been added to the calendar.

YOM HA-SHOA HOLOCAUST MEMORIAL DAY

When Is It?

Yom Ha-Shoa, Holocaust Memorial Day, is the 27th day of the Jewish month of Nissan. (Passover concludes on the 22nd of Nissan, so it will typically occur during April.) It is also common to incorporate some level of Holocaust memorial into the observance of the 9th of Av, because that is the most challenging day of the Jewish calendar.

What Is the Reason for This Commemoration?

We remember the six million Jews murdered during the Holocaust. As the years pass and the number of Holocaust survivors dwindle, it is important to hear the remaining Holocaust survivors give their eyewitness accounts. I believe it's important for young adults and age appropriate children to hear this "testimony" as well. All Birthright group trips include a visit to Yad Vashem, the Holocaust Memorial Museum in Jerusalem, and whenever possible, a live audience with a Holocaust survivor.

Yad Vashem Hall of Names by David Shankbone.jpg

YOM HA-ATZMAUT
(ISRAEL) INDEPENDENCE DAY

When Is It?

Yom Ha-atzmaut, Israel's Independence Day, is the 5th day of the Jewish month of Iyar (approximately two weeks after Passover).

What Is the Reason for This Commemoration?

This day commemorates the day in 1948 when the modern State of Israel came into existence. The creation of Israel was the first Jewish autonomy in the land of Israel in almost two thousand years.

YOM YERUSHALAYIM
JERUSALEM DAY

When Is It?

Yom Yerushalayim, Jerusalem Day, is the 28th day of the Jewish month of Iyar (approximately six weeks after Passover and one week prior to Shavuot).

What Is the Reason for This Commemoration?

This day commemorates the 1967 liberation of the half of Jerusalem held by the Jordanians, including the Western Wall. Israel's stunning victory against the collective might of several Arab armies during the Six Day War, was one of the greatest military victories of all time, and the stories of grown men weeping upon reaching "The Wall" are among the most moving.

Simply Jewish

CHAPTER FIVE:
Kosher

KOSHER

A popular misconception is that "kosher food" is food that has been "blessed by the Rabbi". The Torah; (Leviticus 11:1-11:23), prohibits eating certain types of foods, and establishes criteria for foods that may be eaten. The foods that are permitted to be eaten are called kosher, which means 'properly prepared' in Hebrew.

What is the Reason for Keeping Kosher?

The kosher laws are observed because the Torah explicitly establishes keeping kosher as a mitzvah. Many commentators have explained that the rationale for "keeping kosher" is the impact that food has on you. As Ludwig Feuerbach wrote in 1863, "Man is what he eats", which later evolved into, "You are what you eat." Today, we know that what we eat has a vital impact on our physical health. The Torah teaches us that what we eat also has a vital impact on our spiritual health. Eating kosher food aids spiritual growth, while ingesting non-kosher food is an obstacle to spiritual growth.

How Do You "Keep Kosher"?

The laws of kosher are explained in more detail in, *Kosher for the Clueless but Curious: A Fun, Fact-Filled, and Spiritual Guide to All Things Kosher*, by Rabbi Shimon Apisdorf. To succinctly summarize: The food product must be kosher and the kosher item must be prepared in a way that does not render it non-kosher.

Kosher Fish, Kosher Fowl, Kosher Animals

For a fish to be kosher it must have fins and scales. Salmon is in, but lobster is out.

The Torah did not list specific physical characteristics for a fowl to be deemed kosher, and only listed the non-kosher species. The only species of fowl that are deemed to be kosher are the few that we have - an unbroken tradition that certifies that the species is kosher.

For an animal to be kosher it must have split hooves and chew its cud (ruminate). Therefore, steak, a product of a cow, is in, but bacon, a product of a pig, is way out.

Preparing Kosher Food

But is steak always 'in'? Well, not so fast. Not only must the animal be a kosher animal, it must also be ritually slaughtered, ('schechted'). If the cow was not ritually slaughtered, the steak is not kosher. (Even if properly slaughtered, not all parts of the cow are kosher).

Additionally, kosher food can't be mixed with other (non-kosher) foods. It can't be prepared with, or in, non-kosher utensils or cooked in a non-kosher oven.

One more thing - the Torah prohibits mixing dairy and meat. Thus, topping a 100% kosher hamburger, with a 100% kosher slice of cheese, will make a 100% "traif" (not kosher) cheeseburger.

Mixing Meat and Dairy Products

The prohibition against mixing meat and dairy products extends beyond eating hamburgers and other foods that have meat and dairy mixed together. Once a person eats meat products, he is required to wait before eating a dairy meal, so that they don't mix during the digestive process. The most prevalent custom is to wait six hours. The custom does vary, and Jews of German descent, wait only three hours. The reason for waiting between meals is to allow the meat to be fully digested. Since dairy products are digested more quickly, a waiting period is not necessary prior to enjoying a meat meal. It is sufficient to merely rinse your mouth.

What Does "Glatt Kosher" Mean?

The term "glatt kosher" is a certification that the animal is kosher according to the more exacting standards. For an animal to be kosher, it must have been "viable" at the time of slaughter. Today, most cows have lungs that are impaired in a manner that makes viability unlikely. When the lungs of the cow are checked and certified as healthy, the cow may be certified as glatt kosher.

Why Did My Kosher Observant Friend Look So Uncomfortable When I Baked a Kosher Cake for Her?

Ah yes, Jewish guilt. On the one hand, your friend appreciated your effort and friendship, and did not want to offend you.

On the other hand, she was probably very concerned whether the cake was actually kosher. Yes, you used the same exact cake mix that she buys. But what about the other issues? Your utensils, baking pans, and oven need to be kosher as well.

Is "Keeping Kosher" as Difficult as It Seems?

Actually, it has never been easier to keep kosher, as more and more kosher products hit the market every year. Like anything in life, it just takes a little time to learn all the rules.

How Can I Tell Which Products Are Kosher?

As we noted earlier, certain animals and fish are kosher. Fruits and vegetables always start out kosher, but some like spinach and broccoli are prone to insect infestation and must be washed prior to eating. But what happens when the always-kosher tomato is just one ingredient in a tomato sauce? What about the hundreds of products sold in the supermarket; how can you tell if they are kosher?

It is very difficult to pick up a box of cookies or cake mix, or a "South Beach Diet Meal Replacement Bar", and know if the twenty or more listed ingredients are all kosher. Certainly, when the listed ingredients include things like "maltodextrin" or "artificial flavors", without specifying what those flavors are, determining kosher status is well beyond the ken of most consumers.

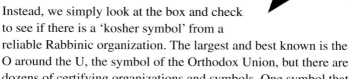

Instead, we simply look at the box and check to see if there is a 'kosher symbol' from a reliable Rabbinic organization. The largest and best known is the O around the U, the symbol of the Orthodox Union, but there are dozens of certifying organizations and symbols. One symbol that is meaningless is a plain "k". In most states, any company is allowed to put a "k" on a label, and it does not mean there is any Rabbinic certification that the product is kosher.

CHAPTER SIX:

Jewish Ritual Items

The "ritual items" discussed in this
chapter include items used only at
specific times, such as Tefilin, items
that are in constant use, such as
the mezuzah, and well recognized
symbols, like the Star of David.

Excluded from this chapter are items
that fit better in other chapters, like
the menorah, which is discussed in the
Chanukah section of Chapter Three.

KIPPA

(pronounced key-pah)

What is a Kippa and Why is it Worn?

A Kippa, also referred to as a skullcap, (or
Yarmulka in Yiddish), is a head covering.
It is worn as a sign of respect for, and
acknowledgement
of, 'God', Who is
above us.

Since the objective is to
cover the head, kippot (plural
for kippa) can be made of
any material; and hats, even
baseball caps, attain the same
objective.

Knitted Kippa

Interestingly enough, wearing a Kippa is not a Biblical commandment.
Nonetheless, it has become, perhaps, the most obvious symbol that the
wearer is a practicing Jew.

How Do You Wear It?

Kippot should fit comfortably and should
cover the majority of the
head. Kippot come
in many sizes,
colors, and
styles.

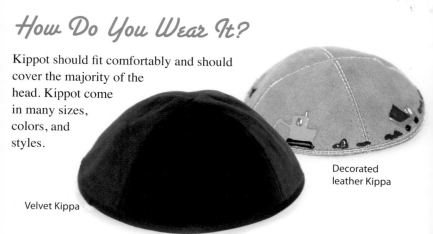

Decorated
leather Kippa

Velvet Kippa

There's usually a box of standard black or white ones available at synagogues and weddings. If you don't want to "look like a rookie", consider bringing your own. Kippot are available at Judaica shops or online.

If you plan to wear one out of the kippa box, bring some bobby pins or clips to keep the "one size fits none" kippa in place. See the photos for some examples of different kinds of kippot.

Who Wears a Kippa?

Today, it is normative practice for men and boys over three years old to have their heads covered during all waking hours. If an individual does not cover his head all day, it would be appropriate to cover his head when reciting a blessing, while engaging in a ritual, or while attending a synagogue. Men who are not Jewish are not required to wear kippot, but may do so as a sign of friendship or respect while attending a Jewish ritual or ceremony. Women are not required to wear kippot.

Why Don't Women Wear Kippot?

If we return to the creation of the Jewish Nation at Mount Sinai some 3,600 years ago, it is clear that it was not normative practice for men to wear kippot. The practice evolved over time and was a specific response to a uniquely male problem, the lack of awe of Heaven. Thus, far from "dissing" women, excluding them from wearing kippot is actually a great compliment, as it acknowledges that women don't have the same need to increase their intuitive "awe of Heaven".

Paper Kippa

STAR OF DAVID

What Is a Star of David?

The Star of David, or Magen Dovid (shield of David) is the six pointed star made of interlocking triangles that has become universally recognized as a Jewish symbol.

This symbol adorns the flag of the modern state of Israel. According to legend, the Star of David can be traced back some three thousand years, to the time of King David, whose soldiers used shields that were also adorned with this symbol. According to other views, the shields themselves were shaped with six points and resembled the Star of David.

Does the Star of David Have Any Religious Significance?

No. The Star of David does not have any religious significance per se, as it is not part of any rite, ritual or custom. Nonetheless, Kabbalists (Rabbis who taught Jewish mysticism, called "Kabbalah") have noted that the six points in the star point in every direction; north, east, south, west, up and down, symbolizing God's presence in every direction. The importance of the Star of David is symbolic as a source of Jewish unity and pride, and as a reminder of where we can find God, if we would only look.

Being a Real Star of David.

Buying a beautiful silver Star of David is the easy part. Wearing it publicly and proudly is a wonderful demonstration of Jewish pride. But the real goal is not just to wear it, it's to live it; to learn more about our heritage, and to try to make a positive impact on society, being "a light unto the nations" (Isaiah 42:6).

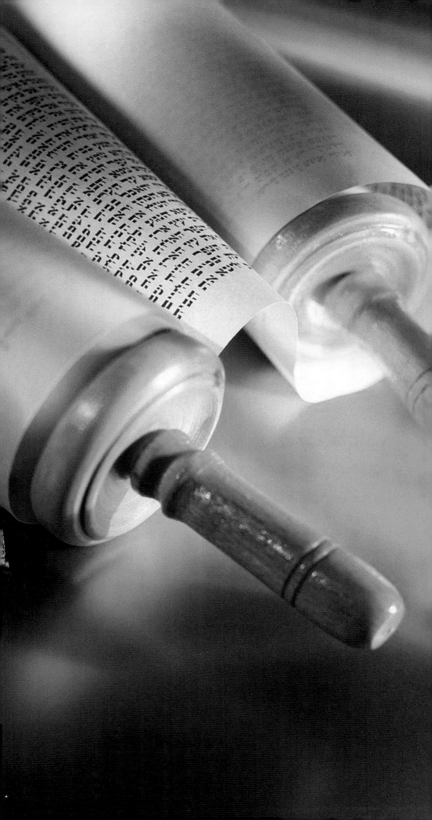

TORAH SCROLL

What Is the Torah?

The Torah (pronounced toe-rah) is the common name for the Five Books of the Bible: Genesis, Exodus, Leviticus, Numbers, and Deuteronomy.

A scribe writes the five books on parchment and this becomes the Torah Scroll that is read in synagogue. Each week a different "Torah Reading" is read, and the entire Torah is completed annually.

More broadly, the term "Torah" may also include the books of the Prophets, the Talmud, and all other types of authentic Jewish teachings. (Please see the "Three Pillars" for more detail.)

Torah Insider

Jews have always had great reverence for the Torah Scroll. Typically, the Torah Scroll is kept in an ornate ark. When the ark is opened, the congregation stands. When the Torah is carried from the ark, it is customary to try and kiss it as it goes by. What is the reason for the

reverence for the Torah? The Torah is not only Divinely authored, it is the blueprint for the knowledge, wisdom and morality that God wishes to impart. When Jews are referred to as "the People of the Book", the Torah is the book referred to.

PRAYER BOOKS:
THE SIDDUR & THE MACHZOR

What Is a Siddur?

The Jewish prayer book is known as a "siddur" (pronounced sid'or, plural siddurim). It is called a siddur because it puts the prayers into order, or "seder" in Hebrew.

The holiday version of the siddur is called a "machzor" (pronounced mach'zor, plural machzorim). The name is derived from the root "chozer", "to return". As the holidays return to us annually, we, hopefully, return to them as well. Today, prayer books translated from the original Hebrew in just about every language are available at Jewish book stores or online.

Isn't It Better if I Say a Short Prayer Spontaneously, Instead of the One-Size-Fits-All Prayer in the Siddur?

An excellent question. We discuss praying in more detail in the chapter titled "The Three Pillars". But to succinctly answer the question, note that the prayers in the siddur were never meant to replace a person's spontaneous heart-felt prayers; they were meant to supplement them. Additionally, most people are not really capable of authoring their own prayers, and without the siddur, they would be left without any means of praying.

TALIT

(pronounced ta-leet)

What is a Talit?

A Talit is a special cloak worn during the morning prayer service, (and by the Chazan/Prayer Leader at other services).

Usually, Jewish men start wearing a Talit after marriage, although some have the custom to start wearing a Talit upon becoming a Bar Mitzvah. and in the Sephardic communities boys start wearing a talit as soon as they are mature enough to understand the commandment. A Talit has four corners and each corner has special woolen fringes called tzitzit (see the next section).

A Talit is often referred to as a 'prayer shawl' although that term suggests that the Talit may be worn around the neck. In fact, it is intended to be worn more like a cape than a scarf.

Here's How to Put on a Talit:

1. Take the Talit with both hands, 'extending' it fully, so that you can see the collar band (atarah), (upon which the blessing is often embroidered).

2. Recite the blessing: *Blessed are You, Ado-noy*, our God, King of the Universe, Who has made us holy with His commandments and commanded us to wrap ourselves with tzitzit.* The blessing is reproduced in Hebrew, English and transliterated in Chapter 9.

3. Wrap yourself in the Talit by putting it over your head and swinging it around your shoulder. Afterwards, the Talit is worn draped on the shoulders, in the proper manner.

Why Are There Black Stripes on the Talit?

For the record, it should be noted that although black stripes are customary in most Ashkenazic communities, they are not 'required' and some have blue stripes, colorful stripes, or no stripes at all. The reason

for the black stripes is unclear. It has been suggested that the stripes were originally blue, as a reminder of the time when the fringes were dyed blue (when soaked in a liquid extracted from a now unknown fish). It is possible that sometime during the middle ages when Jews were forbidden to wear the royal color of blue, the stripes were changed to black. to serve as a subtle, but frequent reminder of our loss of the Temple and our exile.

TZITZIT

(pronounced tzee-zeet)

What Are They?

Tzitzit are the woolen fringes worn at the corners of four-cornered garments. Tzitzit are attached to a Talit and Talit Katan, (see the next section), with eight strands of wool and using five knots.

Why Are Tzitzit Worn?

The numerical value of the word Tzitzit (600), plus the eight strands and five knots equals 613. Wearing Tzitzit is intended to remind us of the 613 mitzvot (positive deeds we should perform and negative deeds we must avoid) contained in the Torah. As it explicitly says in the Torah, "These shall be your Tzitzit, and when you see them you shall remember all of God's commandments"; (Numbers 15:39).

A classic incident is recorded in the Talmud; (Menachot 43(b). A certain young man made a visit to a particularly beautiful woman, a practitioner of the world's oldest profession. As he was quickly disrobing, he was inadvertently smacked in the face by the woolen fringes. At that moment, despite the woman's great beauty being displayed so vividly, he changed his mind.

TALIT KATAN

(pronounced ta-leet ka-tahn)

What is it?

As a practical matter, when people talk today about "wearing Tzitzit", they really mean a Talit Katan. As noted previously, Tzitzit are the fringes worn on four-cornered garments.

This is an actual Biblical command; (Numbers 15:38). Today, most people don't own many four-cornered garments. They have been out of style for the last couple of thousand years, and it is probably safe to say they won't be coming back into fashion any time soon. We could easily conclude that we are exempt from this mitzvah. However, as the Talit Katan demonstrates so beautifully, we are not looking for exemptions; we are looking for mitzvot. It is customary to wear a 'Talit Katan', a four cornered garment especially made to fulfill the Biblical requirements. It is typically worn between the shirt and undershirt, although many Chasidim, (Jews that wear long black frocks and black hats), wear them above the shirt.

Recently, while I was changing at my health club, a man noticed my Talit Katan and asked about it. After my brief explanation, he concluded, "it seems like a hassle". I don't think so. We believe that every step you take wearing a Talit Katan is a 'mitzvah', a Biblically commanded positive deed. How many steps do you take every day? If you believe we are here to do mitzvot, they just don't get easier than this. What may seem like a 'hassle' to some people, is actually 'low lying fruit' to others.

The Talit Katan is worn daily and the following blessing is recited when putting them on in the morning: *Blessed are You, Ado-noy, our God, King of the Universe, Who has made us holy with His commandments and commanded us to wrap ourselves with Tzitzit.* The blessing is reproduced in Hebrew, English and transliterated in Chapter 9.

TEFILIN

(pronounced Tuh-fill-in)

What Are They?

Tefilin, (phylacteries), are two small black boxes. Inside Tefilin are four parchments upon which are written four paragraphs from the Torah, (including the well known, vitally important "Shemah Yisrael"). The Tefilin are kept in place with leather straps.

Wearing Tefilin is a Biblical mitzvah (Exodus 13:16). Today, Tefilin are worn during weekday morning prayers. Earlier generations actually wore Tefilin the entire day. (Usage is now limited to the time of morning prayers because we are not capable of maintaining the proper decorum during the entire day.) Tefilin are meant to be a symbol of our relationship with God. They are not worn on Shabbat because the entire day of Shabbat is already a symbol, and no further symbol is required. It is also worth noting that the Talmud records the statement of the great sage Raish Lakeesh, "Whoever puts on Tefilin will live long"; (Menachot 44(b). The Talmudic sage Rabbah went even further, "Whoever wears Tefilin with a Talit and says Shemah... is promised a place in the World to Come".

How Are They Worn?

One box of the Tefilin is worn on the head, above the forehead. The other is worn on the upper arm, opposite the heart. It would be fair to note that the placement on the head, the source of intellect, and the arm, the source of our strength, is not a coincidence.

How to Put on Tefilin:

Roll up your sleeve. (If you are a righty roll up your left sleeve, if

a lefty, roll up your right sleeve.) Remove watches and rings on that hand.

Take the 'hand Tefilin' (*shel yad*) out of its case and unwind the leather straps. Open the 'loop' as much as needed so that you can slide the hand Tefilin all the way up your arm, until it rests on your biceps.

Now, with the hand Tefilin sitting at the center of your bicep, recite the first blessing, *Blessed are You, Ado-noy, our God, King of the Universe, Who has made us holy with His commandments, and commanded us to put on Tefilin.* (The blessings are reproduced in Hebrew, English and spelled phonetically in Chapter 9).

Tighten the loop and start wrapping the leather strap around your arm.
Wrap once around the biceps. Wrap seven times around your lower arm between the biceps through the end of your wrist, and then temporarily wind around the wrist or palm. At this point pause and take out and unwrap the head Tefilin.

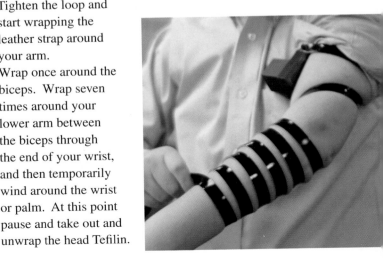

Place the 'head Tefilin' (*shel rosh*) on your head. It should be placed exactly at the center of your head, just above your (original) hairline.

The head Tefilin should be adjusted so that the knot is centered, at the back of your head, on the bone at the bottom of your skull, which is typically at eye level.

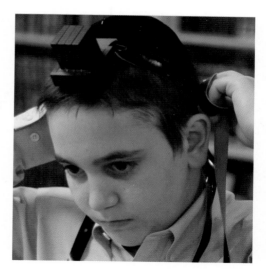

Recite the second blessing: *Blessed are You, Ado-noy, our God, King of the Universe, Who has made us holy with His commandments, and commanded concerning the mitzvah of Tefilin.*

Adjust the head straps. Make sure they are facing black side up and tuck them into your belt to conveniently keep them in place.

Return to the hand Tefilin straps. Wrap once around the hand, three times around the middle finger, around the fourth finger, back around the hand over and over until there is no strap remaining.

Tuck the remainder in under the middle strap to keep it in place.

MEZUZAH

(pronounced meh-zoo-zah)

A dead giveaway that you are entering a Jewish home is the small rectangular box on the right side of the doorpost. This box is called a 'mezuzah.'

Putting a mezuzah on your door is a Biblical mitzvah; (Deuteronomy 6:9). Although the outside can be made of any material, it is often ornate, made of silver or handcrafted. This is done to perform the mitzvah in the most appealing fashion, thereby demonstrating our love for the mitzvot.

שְׁמַ֖ע יִשְׂרָאֵ֑ל יְדֹוָֽד אֱלֹדֵ֖ינוּ יְדֹוָ֖ד אֶחָ֑ד וְאָהַבְתָּ֗ אֵ֛ת יְדֹוָ֖ד אֱלֹדֶ֑יךָ בְּכָל־לְבָֽבְךָ֖ וּבְכָל־נַפְשְׁךָ֖ וּבְכָל־מְאֹדֶֽךָ וְהָי֞וּ הַדְּבָרִ֤ים הָאֵ֨לֶּה֙ אֲשֶׁ֨ר אָנֹכִ֤י מְצַוְּךָ֖ הַיּ֑וֹם עַל־לְבָבֶֽךָ וְשִׁנַּנְתָּ֤ם לְבָנֶ֨יךָ֙ וְדִבַּרְתָּ֖ בָּ֑ם בְּשִׁבְתְּךָ֤ בְּבֵיתֶ֨ךָ֙ וּבְלֶכְתְּךָ֖ בַדֶּ֔רֶךְ וּבְשָׁכְבְּךָ֖ וּבְקוּמֶֽךָ וּקְשַׁרְתָּ֖ם לְא֣וֹת עַל־יָדֶ֑ךָ וְהָי֥וּ לְטֹטָפֹ֖ת בֵּ֣ין עֵינֶֽיךָ וּכְתַבְתָּ֖ם עַל־מְזֻז֣וֹת בֵּיתֶ֑ךָ וּבִשְׁעָרֶֽיךָ וְהָיָ֗ה אִם־שָׁמֹ֤עַ תִּשְׁמְעוּ֙ אֶל־מִצְוֺתַ֔י אֲשֶׁ֧ר אָנֹכִ֛י מְצַוֶּ֥ה אֶתְכֶ֖ם הַיּ֑וֹם לְאַהֲבָ֞ה אֶת־יְדֹוָ֤ד אֱלֹֽדֵיכֶם֙ וּלְעָבְד֔וֹ בְּכָל־לְבַבְכֶ֖ם וּבְכָל־נַפְשְׁכֶֽם וְנָתַתִּ֥י מְטַֽר־אַרְצְכֶ֖ם בְּעִתּ֑וֹ יוֹרֶ֣ה וּמַלְק֑וֹשׁ וְאָסַפְתָּ֣ דְגָנֶ֔ךָ וְתִירֹֽשְׁךָ֖ וְיִצְהָרֶֽךָ וְנָתַתִּ֛י עֵ֥שֶׂב בְּשָׂדְךָ֖ לִבְהֶמְתֶּ֑ךָ וְאָכַלְתָּ֖ וְשָׂבָֽעְתָּ הִשָּֽׁמְר֣וּ לָכֶ֔ם פֶּ֥ן יִפְתֶּ֖ה לְבַבְכֶ֑ם וְסַרְתֶּ֗ם וַעֲבַדְתֶּם֙ אֱלֹדִ֣ים אֲחֵרִ֔ים וְהִשְׁתַּחֲוִיתֶ֖ם לָהֶֽם וְחָרָ֨ה אַף־יְדֹוָ֜ד בָּכֶ֗ם וְעָצַ֤ר אֶת־הַשָּׁמַ֨יִם֙ וְלֹא־יִהְיֶ֣ה מָטָ֔ר וְהָ֣אֲדָמָ֔ה לֹ֥א תִתֵּ֖ן אֶת־יְבוּלָ֑הּ וַאֲבַדְתֶּ֣ם מְהֵרָ֗ה מֵעַל֙ הָאָ֣רֶץ הַטֹּבָ֔ה אֲשֶׁ֥ר יְדֹוָ֖ד נֹתֵ֥ן לָכֶֽם וְשַׂמְתֶּ֞ם אֶת־דְּבָרַ֤י אֵ֨לֶּה֙ עַל־לְבַבְכֶ֖ם וְעַֽל־נַפְשְׁכֶ֑ם וּקְשַׁרְתֶּ֨ם אֹתָ֤ם לְאוֹת֙ עַל־יֶדְכֶ֔ם וְהָי֥וּ לְטוֹטָפֹ֖ת בֵּ֣ין עֵינֵיכֶֽם וְלִמַּדְתֶּ֥ם אֹתָ֛ם אֶת־בְּנֵיכֶ֖ם לְדַבֵּ֣ר בָּ֑ם בְּשִׁבְתְּךָ֤ בְּבֵיתֶ֨ךָ֙ וּבְלֶכְתְּךָ֣ בַדֶּ֔רֶךְ וּבְשָׁכְבְּךָ֖ וּבְקוּמֶֽךָ וּכְתַבְתָּ֛ם עַל־מְזוּז֥וֹת בֵּיתֶ֖ךָ וּבִשְׁעָרֶֽיךָ לְמַ֨עַן יִרְבּ֜וּ יְמֵיכֶ֗ם וִימֵ֤י בְנֵיכֶם֙ עַ֚ל הָֽאֲדָמָ֔ה אֲשֶׁ֨ר נִשְׁבַּ֧ע יְדֹוָ֛ד לַאֲבֹתֵיכֶ֖ם לָתֵ֣ת לָהֶ֑ם כִּימֵ֥י הַשָּׁמַ֖יִם עַל־הָאָֽרֶץ

Far more important than the decorative case is the inside of the mezuzah. Inside the mezuzah is a parchment upon which is written important sections from the Torah, the "Shemah Yisrael/Hear Israel", our declaration of faith (see Chapter 9 for full text); as well as the commandment to affix a mezuzah.

The mezuzah serves to remind us of who we are meant to be, both when we are entering and exiting our home. There is a longstanding custom to kiss the mezuzah every time you walk by. (We also kiss the Torah as it goes by and kiss our holy books when opening and closing them. This custom is meant to demonstrate our affection for these holy items.)

How to Affix a Mezuzah

The mezuzah is attached on the right doorpost as you enter the room, about two-thirds of the way up. The mezuzah is affixed to the doorpost on an angle.

At the time you put up a mezuzah, you say the following blessing: *Blessed are You, Ado-noy, our God, King of the Universe, Who has made us holy with His commandments, and commanded us to affix Mezuzot.*

The blessing is reproduced in Hebrew, English and is transliterated in Chapter 9.

The photo above demonstrates the proper placement of a mezuzah. The photo on the previous page shows the parchment that is inserted into the mezuzah.

Why Is the Mezuzah Placed on an Angle?

Originally, there was a debate regarding the proper placement of a mezuzah. One opinion was that the mezuzah should be placed parallel to the doorpost; the other opinion was that the mezuzah should be placed perpendicular to the doorpost. It was decided to compromise and put the mezuzah on an angle, and this would serve as a constant reminder that loving homes are filled with compromise.

CHAPTER SEVEN:

The Three Pillars

In a perfect world, this would be the first chapter, because this chapter contains the 'soul' of Judaism. The rituals and mitzvot we discuss in chapter one are important, but this chapter tells us what Judaism has to say about the 'big picture'.

Pirkay Avot (1:2), the classic "Ethics of the Fathers" states that "the world stands on three pillars, on Torah, Avodah (prayer), and Kindness". Without these three, the world could not exist. Let's examine each.

TORAH

What is Torah?

One of the most important but least known mitzvot is the mitzvah to "study Torah". When we say "Torah", we mean both the written law and the oral law. The Five Books of Moses and the Books of Prophets are the written law; and the Mishna and Talmud are the oral law. The Torah also includes explanations on all of the above, as well as works that explain Jewish law and tradition.

"Hey, Why is the Oral Law written"?

Good question. Originally, for many generations, the oral law, which was also given to Moses on Mount Sinai, was transmitted orally from parent to child and teacher to student. As Jews suffered persecution, it was feared that the ability to faithfully transmit these lessons would be diminished. During a temporary lull in the era of the Roman persecutions, "Rabbi Yehuda, the Prince", gathered all the Rabbis and assembled 'the Mishna', as a condensed form of the oral law. This was later expanded into 'the Talmud'.

Why is Studying Torah So Important?

We know we are here in this world for a reason. How do we know what that reason is? How do we know what is good and what is bad? Should each person define what is right and what is wrong by their own standards? What if on one block you have one person who feels 'taking' small amounts from big corporations is not really bad? Next door, you have a man who is horrified at the idea of taking even a penny that does not belong to him, but has no problem having a relationship with a woman who is unhappily married. The third neighbor would never commit adultery that violates his own personal rules of behavior, but he is an underworld leader; and although he would always hold the door for ladies, he has no problem facilitating the (permanent) disappearance of a rival. A fourth neighbor would neither steal, nor kill, nor commit adultery, yet he has no problem verbally assaulting others. A fifth neighbor would never hurt a fly, but he takes great delight in gossiping about everyone else in the neighborhood. The sixth neighbor is universally described as a good guy who donates half his salary to charity. Despite being solicited by people who have no money to feed their children, he feels the only charity worth supporting is the "Society for the Preservation of the Greater Prairie Chicken".

What is right and what is wrong is very difficult to determine on our own. Especially during our youth, but really throughout life, we are pulled by many interests and desires. We are all greatly influenced by our friends, family and society. Without proper guidance the unaided human intellect can easily be led away from and can't completely fathom that which is truly good.

The Torah is God's instruction book on how to live a good, happy and moral life. When you bought your first computer, did you look at the instruction manual? G-d created us and we are far more complex than any computer. Shouldn't we read the instruction manual? The reason studying Torah is so important is because it is the way for us to find out about the 'manufacturer's recommendations'.

Can't You Live Without the Instruction Manual?

I'm reminded of the time I purchased a barbecue grill and assembled it without bothering to read the instructions. I was able to do it, but it took a very long time. The task was more complicated than it needed to be, and I was left with a whole bunch of extra parts that I could not figure out what to do with. (Oh, and the grill never really worked as well as it should have).

How to Study Torah

There is certainly a lot to study, but don't be discouraged; even studying a little makes a big difference. The key is setting aside a set time dedicated for Torah study. It could be a set time every day or it could be a set time every week. There are many people who study the

weekly Torah portion every week with commentaries and complete the entire Torah in a year; others study one page of Talmud every day and finish the Talmud in seven and a half years.

I particularly like the Partners in Torah weekly program, where people who are interested pick any Jewish study topic and are introduced to a volunteer mentor with whom they study on a weekly basis, either in person, on the phone or online. I have had study partners who have requested topics as diverse as learning how to read Hebrew, learning about Jewish holidays and customs, learning Ethics of the Fathers, the weekly Torah reading, and even detailed text-based studies. (For contact information, see Recommended Resources)   Many synagogues and organizations offer classes and lectures. (see Recommended Resources) If I had to pick one presentation as a 'must see' it would be "Discovery", by Aish HaTorah, because it presents the truth of Torah in an intelligent and entertaining manner.

AVODAH PRAYER

The second, and in some ways the most controversial of the three pillars is "Avodah", roughly translated as prayer and belief in God. As we discussed in the High Holiday section, God, who is omnipotent, does not need our prayers. We need our prayers. We need prayers of thanks to demonstrate we are an appreciative people. We need prayers of hope to demonstrate we are a hopeful people. We need to know that regardless of how hopeless a situation may appear, our Father in Heaven can intercede on our behalf. As the Talmud (Brachot 10b) says, "Even when you feel the sword on your neck, it is never too late to pray". We need the daily prayers, particularly the Amidah, since that tells us what we should be praying for.

In a nutshell, most people view prayer as trying to change God's mind. The truth is, prayer should be about changing us, changing who we are and perhaps thereby changing how we relate to God and how God relates to us.

How to Pray

Let's face it. Most people just don't like praying. People are either put off by the whole idea of God needing our prayers (which we have dealt with), or find the prayers uninteresting and boring. I offer the following suggestions to try to enhance the experience:

- Know what you are saying. Obviously, praying in Hebrew if you can read Hebrew, but don't understand a word, is not going to be a very rewarding experience. A good first step would be obtaining a translated prayer book or siddur. I would suggest The Complete ArtScroll Siddur or The Complete Metsudah Siddur.

- Less is more. Certainly for a beginner, praying a little and concentrating, is better than whipping through the whole siddur. The two most important prayers are "Shemah Yisrael", (conveniently, a short declaration of our faith) and the Amidah/ Shemona Esray.

- Make it personal. The prayers were set long ago in recognition of the fact that people can't spontaneously make up their own prayers. But they were meant to be a minimum. If you want to add to your prayers based on what is in your heart, it is not only appropriate, it is beautiful.

- Imagine you are actually talking to God. Besides the not infrequent complaint that praying can be boring, I have actually witnessed people praying the silent Amidah prayer while chewing gum and/ or checking to see who is calling on their cell phone. If you had a problem and were granted five minutes with the President, how would you spend those five minutes? If you are wise, you would use that time as efficiently as possible. You would surely mention your appreciation for favors the President has already done for you, continue with your request, and then conclude by expressing your appreciation for the opportunity to be heard. You are unlikely to be chewing gum, checking your cell phone, or feeling bored. Remembering that we are praying to God is both the most difficult and most important part of praying.

KINDNESS

The third and final pillar upon which the world rests is "kindness". Judaism has always put a great emphasis on acts of kindness. God is kind and we are bid to emulate God and be kind. Although this certainly includes the obligation to tithe and give charity, charity is only one example. Additionally, we are bid to visit the sick, comfort mourners, attend to the deceased, care for widows and orphans, and welcome strangers, as well as other acts of kindness.

The good news is that involvement in social causes and charity is something that Jews still retain. The bad news is that without the first pillar, "learning Torah", the selection of causes and charities has not always been in the priority the Torah would dictate.

How To Give Tzedaka/ Charity

The laws of the priority of Jewish charitable giving are complex.
A few rules:

- Ten percent. The general obligation is to tithe, that is, to give ten percent of your "net income". For example, if your business grosses $150,000 and nets $100,000, and you pay $30,000 in income taxes, you should give 10% of the remaining $70,000 to Tzedaka. ('High earners', which we won't attempt to define, are encouraged to give as much as 20%.)

- 'Real' charity. The rules for giving 'Tzedaka' are not the same rules applied by the IRS. An individual can be a patron of the arts and donate generously to museums and receive a nice tax deduction. That amount would not count towards the obligation to tithe. Nor would the contribution to the "Society for the Protection of the Greater Prairie Chicken", that we mentioned above. These other causes may be worthwhile. However, "Tzedaka" (derived from the word 'Tzedek' which means 'righteous'), obligates us to be righteous, and as the verse says, (Deuteronomy 15:8) we must "open our hands" and not ignore the plight of our indigent brothers and sisters.

- People who are indigent come first. Supporting Jewish institutions is also Tzedaka, but great care must be exerted in determining how much to give which institution. Tomchei Shabbos is an organization that has volunteers discreetly deliver packages of food late Thursday night to unemployed and indigent people. To avoid embarrassing the recipients, they place the food on the front door, knock and leave. This is a very high form of Tzedaka/ charity. Donating to a scholarship fund that allows a child from a poor family to receive a Jewish education that she would not otherwise be able to receive, or helping fund an orphan's wedding, are also very worthy. Donating to synagogues is important too. Nonetheless, if you had a million dollars to give to Tzedaka and you gave it all to the synagogue and nothing to poor people, you may have met the letter of the law, but violated the spirit of the law.

- Concentric circles. Our first obligation is to support our immediate family if they are in need. Next, we work our way out to extended family, our community and the poor of the Land of Israel, and finally other communities.

God's Special Promise

Generally, we are bid to have faith and not to 'test' God. The one exception is charity. We are told that if we give charity as we are supposed to, God guarantees that we will come out way ahead. (See Talmud, tractate Tanit 9, Tur/Shulchan Aruch 247.)

Charity Saves From Death

In addition to the reasons we have already discussed for giving charity, there is another important reason - it protects the donor.

The Talmud, (Bava Batra, quoting Proverbs 10:2) states that "charity saves from death". One story that vividly demonstrates this point involves the daughter of the great Talmudic sage, Rabbi Akiva. On her wedding day, upon hearing the pleas of a hungry beggar, the young woman interrupted her wedding preparations, pinned her ornate wedding headpiece to the wall, and brought food to the hungry man. Upon her return, she discovered that the pin killed a large snake. Giving charity literally saved her life. It makes perfect sense. Although we often don't see it, God runs the world in a way that is often described as 'measure for measure', meaning that as we treat other people, God treats us. When you deal charitably with a poor person, God responds in kind.

Acts of Kindness

In addition to giving charity, the Torah recognizes other types of acts of kindness.

Visiting the Sick

Not only is it a mitzvah to visit the sick, the Talmud states that it is a mitzvah "without limit", and "someone who visits the sick is spared from the judgment of hell". (Nedarim 40a)

Why is visiting the sick so important?

The Talmud states that "visiting a sick person removes one-sixtieth of the illness". (Nedarim 39b) A visit from a friend or relative can make the difference between life and death. Positive encouragement and demonstrations of love and support can give the ill person new resolve to live and to fight the illness. The one caveat is to be sensitive to the needs of the sick person. During the holiday of Sukkot, you can pretty much pick up a lulav and fulfill the mitzvah anytime you wish. However, you can only visit the sick at times when the visit is beneficial. Sometimes, the act of kindness is to *not* visit the sick person.

Comforting Mourners and Burying the Dead

Both are vivid examples of kindness, the mitzvah to help someone when they most need help. Each is described in more detail in Chapter 3, Lifecycle Events.

The Greatest Kindness

The greatest kindness you can do is to provide the unemployed with a job. If you can help them before they fall behind on the mortgage and stop bringing in enough food for the family, you will have saved the family much pain and humiliation.

Rescuing Captives

If a fellow Jew is taken captive primarily because he is Jewish, what - if anything - should you do? You should do everything in your power to secure his rescue. Contributing money towards rescuing captives is considered a very high level of charity. What if the ransom demanded is an outrageous amount, and if paid, is likely to result in the targeting of other Jewish victims? The consensus is that it is better not to pay the ransom if doing so will endanger others.

Kindness and Righteousness

Closely related to, and intersecting with the obligation to perform acts of kindness, is the obligation to be righteous. An embezzler that uses his ill-gotten gains to support worthy charities is still an embezzler. The ends do not justify the means. (derived from Deuteronomy 16:20)

A sampling of some of the mitzvot that demonstrate kindness and righteousness follows.

Honoring Your Parents

Honoring and respecting parents actually makes it into the top ten, as in the Ten Commandments, Exodus 20:10. (see sidebar) Why? One of the foundations that Judaism is built upon is that we must be appreciative. The term "Judaism" is derived from Judah, the son of Jacob. Judah's name means "acknowledgement". Judah's mother, Leah, chose this name in appreciation and acknowledgement of God's kindness in blessing her with this son. Being appreciative has always been a top national priority. Whatever level of appreciation you may have for any other person, should pale in comparison to the appreciation you should have for your parents.

Love Your Neighbor

The Torah bids us to "Love your neighbor, as you love yourself." (Leviticus 19:18)

Is that humanly possible? In the fullest sense, it is probably an ideal that we can only aspire to. Nonetheless, we all can genuinely hope and pray for the best to happen to our neighbors, just as we hope and pray for the best for ourselves. Similarly, just as we are very willing to "cut ourselves some slack" when we make a mistake, we should be willing to cut our neighbor some slack as well. The term "neighbor" is defined broadly, and even includes "strangers". We are expressly told to "love the stranger". (Deuteronomy 10:19)

If we must love even strangers, is anything less expected of us regarding our relationships with our spouses, children and siblings?

Neighbors Helping Neighbors

As an extension of loving your neighbor, we should be concerned about his possessions as well. If we see a lost object, we must return it to its rightful owner. (Deuteronomy 22:1-13) According to Jewish law, "Finders, keepers, losers are not weepers". If you see someone struggling with a heavy load, the Torah commands you to help. (Deuteronomy 22:40, Exodus 23:5)

Revenge: A Dish Best Not Served

Directly related to the mitzvah to Love Your Neighbor, are the prohibitions against taking revenge, bearing a grudge, or hating someone in your heart. (Leviticus 19:17-18) We are urged to "rise above". Here's a classic example: your neighbor refuses to lend you his lawn mower and in response, you refuse to lend him your garden hose the following week. For the record, lending him the hose but adding, "Unlike you, who did not lend me your lawn mower, I would be happy to lend you my hose", is still prohibited. This does not mean that you must forego amounts owed to you. Instead, it bars retaliation.

THE 10 COMMANDMENTS
Book of Exodus 19:1-14

1. I am the Transcendent One, your God, Who has taken you out of the land of Egypt, from the house of slavery.

2. You shall not relate to any other gods.

3. Do not take the Name of the Transcendent One, your God, in vain...

4. Remember the Sabbath day in a way that makes it holy...

5. Honor your father and mother...

6. Do not murder.

7. Do not commit adultery.

8. Do not steal or kidnap.

9. Do not testify falsely against a person.

10. Do not covet your friend's house; do not covet your friend's wife...

Don't Cheat

The Torah contains many commandments in this area. They include the following:

- Don't steal and don't rob (Leviticus 19:11-13)
- Don't falsify weights (Leviticus 19:35-36)
- Don't move your neighbor's boundary (Deuteronomy 19:14)
- Pay your workers on time (Deuteronomy 24:15)
- Keep far away from falsehood (Exodus 23:7)

It is interesting to note that the warning to "keep far away" is given for lying and not for the other sins.

Gossip

Another extension of loving your neighbor is the prohibition against being "a tale bearer". (Leviticus, 19:16) People say that "Sticks and stones may break my bones, but names will never harm me." The truth is, our words have tremendous power. They have the potential to heal and comfort or the power to destroy. Saying the wrong thing at the right time can affect the way people are perceived by a potential suitor or employer, or affect their standing among their friends.

CHAPTER EIGHT:

Fact or Fiction?

Jews believe in the Messiah.

FACT. Judaism believes that the Messiah, a descendant of King David, will come either at a predetermined 'outside date' that we are unaware of, or as soon as tomorrow, if we merit it.

Jews believe in the "afterlife".

FACT. Jews believe that after the demise of the body, the soul lives on, and will eventually be reunited with the body at the time of the revival of the dead. Exactly what happens in the "world to come" is subject of differing opinions, but that there is a world to come is one of the principles of our faith.

Jews believe that if you are not Jewish you are damned to eternal hell.

FICTION. Actually, we are unique among the world's major religions. We believe that good, moral, non-Jews can also attain the "world to come". Then, why be Jewish, and have to 'worry' about the burden of 613 mitzvot? Far from being a burden, we believe that having 613 mitzvot gives us more opportunities to not only earn admittance in the world to come, but also gives us the best chance of getting "good seats". Additionally, the mitzvot are God's instructions to us. Fulfilling the mitzvot are our opportunity to do what God deems worthwile.

Judaism believes that the Torah was given privately by God to Moses.

FICTION. God gave the Torah to the Jewish Nation and it was witnessed by every man, woman, and child. This is a critical distinction between Judaism and all other religions. All other religions start with one man having a private audience with God, unwitnessed by any other person.

Judaism believes that if you observe the mitzvot and rituals, you are 'not required' to be kind to others.

FALSE. As we state in the next chapter, The Three Pillars, one of the pillars that the world stands on is "kindness". Additionally, in the Tisha B'Av section we noted that the Temple was destroyed and remains destroyed to this very day, due to the great sin of 'baseless hatred'. Being kind is way up there in importance.

Judaism believes that if you are kind and have a "Jewish heart", but don't partake in any rituals or mitzvot, that is "good enough", because treating people well is what is most important.

FICTION. It is true that being kind to others is vitally important and may well precede the other mitzvot, but it does not replace them. Ideally, we should do both.

According to Jewish law, "finders, keepers, losers, weepers"; you may keep lost objects that you find.

FICTION. Lost objects must be returned to their rightful owner.

According to Jewish law, "sticks and stones may break my bones, but names will never hurt me". In other words, you can't hit anybody, but you are free to say whatever you wish.

FICTION. Jewish Law recognizes that words have the potential to harm, and prohibits name-calling and gossip.

If you have a tattoo you can't be buried in a Jewish cemetery.

FICTION. A number of times young people on Birthright trips (and elsewhere) have asked me the 'tattoo question'. Actually, there are two versions of 'the question'. The second version is, "According to Judaism, is someone with a tattoo permanently banned from Heaven"?

It is true that the Torah bans tattoos (Leviticus 19:28). Our bodies are holy and they are beautiful, and a permanent tattoo mars that holiness and beauty. Does this mean that someone who has a tattoo is going to be denied burial in a Jewish cemetery or banned from Heaven? No. There is a big difference between violating a commandment and being "damned to eternal hell". (Not that we believe in that anyway. Refer to Chapter One and the section "Some basic Jewish beliefs about Death.")

Unfortunately, we live in a time when basic knowledge of our religion is not well-known. Just as people are unaware of the Sabbath and kosher, they are also unaware of the ban on tattoos. Should you get a tattoo? No - according to Jewish law you should not. If you already have one, should you be very worried? I don't think so.

How did this rumor start? Like many rumors, no one seems to know for sure, but one of my students mentioned that she had heard this on a television show. We, as 'the People of the Book', should not be learning about our religion from situation comedies on television.

PART 2

CHAPTER NINE
Ready-to-Use Resources

How can you fully capture 3,600 years of wisdom in less than two hundred pages? You can't. I have attempted to provide a basic understanding of Jewish rites, rituals and customs, in a manner that allows you to perform them, if so inclined. This chapter includes many of the resources you will need.

TRANSLITERATING GUIDE

Throughout this portion of the book, each prayer is "transliterated", Hebrew words are spelled out phonetically allowing English readers to recite the prayers in Hebrew. I know that transliteration is important to some people so I have included it, but don't feel compelled to use it. Reciting prayers in English is perfectly acceptable, as God understands all languages.

Generally, the transliteration spells out words as they sound. However, when the transliterated word, or a part of a word, sounds like an existing English language word, I have opted to use that English word, as the reader will intuitively recognize the word, (for example I transliterate the word in the Shemah prayer "shame" instead of "shaim").

The transliteration follows the pronunciation used predominantly in Israel today.
1. The letters "oo" are pronounced "ew" as in "few".
2. The letter "o" is pronounced like "toe", when it is followed by an "h" or an "e", or ends a word, otherwise it is pronounced like the "o" in "Tom".
3. The letters "ay" are pronounced like "pray".
4. The letters "ch" are pronounced like "Chanukah", not like "change".

RESOURCE I

Blessings On Ritual Items & Shmah Yisrael, The Daily Declaration of Faith

Shemah Yisrael, The Daily Declaration of Faith

Hebrew:

שְׁמַע יִשְׂרָאֵל, יְיָ* אֱלֹהֵינוּ, יְיָ אֶחָד.

בָּרוּךְ שֵׁם כְּבוֹד מַלְכוּתוֹ לְעוֹלָם וָעֶד.

וְאָהַבְתָּ אֵת יְיָ אֱלֹהֶיךָ, בְּכָל לְבָבְךָ, וּבְכָל נַפְשְׁךָ, וּבְכָל מְאֹדֶךָ. וְהָיוּ הַדְּבָרִים הָאֵלֶּה, אֲשֶׁר אָנֹכִי מְצַוְּךָ הַיּוֹם, עַל לְבָבֶךָ. וְשִׁנַּנְתָּם לְבָנֶיךָ, וְדִבַּרְתָּ בָּם, בְּשִׁבְתְּךָ בְּבֵיתֶךָ, וּבְלֶכְתְּךָ בַדֶּרֶךְ, וּבְשָׁכְבְּךָ, וּבְקוּמֶךָ. וּקְשַׁרְתָּם לְאוֹת | עַל יָדֶךָ, וְהָיוּ לְטֹטָפֹת בֵּין עֵינֶיךָ. וּכְתַבְתָּם | עַל מְזֻזוֹת בֵּיתֶךָ וּבִשְׁעָרֶיךָ.

וְהָיָה אִם שָׁמֹעַ תִּשְׁמְעוּ אֶל מִצְוֹתַי, אֲשֶׁר אָנֹכִי מְצַוֶּה אֶתְכֶם הַיּוֹם, לְאַהֲבָה אֵת יְיָ אֱלֹהֵיכֶם וּלְעָבְדוֹ, בְּכָל לְבַבְכֶם וּבְכָל נַפְשְׁכֶם. וְנָתַתִּי מְטַר אַרְצְכֶם בְּעִתּוֹ, יוֹרֶה וּמַלְקוֹשׁ, וְאָסַפְתָּ דְגָנֶךָ, וְתִירֹשְׁךָ וְיִצְהָרֶךָ. וְנָתַתִּי עֵשֶׂב בְּשָׂדְךָ לִבְהֶמְתֶּךָ, וְאָכַלְתָּ וְשָׂבָעְתָּ. הִשָּׁמְרוּ לָכֶם פֶּן יִפְתֶּה לְבַבְכֶם, וְסַרְתֶּם וַעֲבַדְתֶּם אֱלֹהִים אֲחֵרִים וְהִשְׁתַּחֲוִיתֶם לָהֶם. וְחָרָה אַף יְיָ בָּכֶם, וְעָצַר אֶת הַשָּׁמַיִם וְלֹא יִהְיֶה מָטָר, וְהָאֲדָמָה לֹא תִתֵּן אֶת יְבוּלָהּ, וַאֲבַדְתֶּם מְהֵרָה מֵעַל הָאָרֶץ הַטֹּבָה אֲשֶׁר יְיָ נֹתֵן לָכֶם. וְשַׂמְתֶּם אֶת דְּבָרַי אֵלֶּה עַל לְבַבְכֶם וְעַל נַפְשְׁכֶם, וּקְשַׁרְתֶּם אֹתָם לְאוֹת עַל יֶדְכֶם, וְהָיוּ לְטוֹטָפֹת בֵּין עֵינֵיכֶם. וְלִמַּדְתֶּם אֹתָם אֶת בְּנֵיכֶם לְדַבֵּר בָּם, בְּשִׁבְתְּךָ בְּבֵיתֶךָ, וּבְלֶכְתְּךָ בַדֶּרֶךְ, וּבְשָׁכְבְּךָ, וּבְקוּמֶךָ. וּכְתַבְתָּם עַל מְזוּזוֹת בֵּיתֶךָ וּבִשְׁעָרֶיךָ. לְמַעַן יִרְבּוּ יְמֵיכֶם וִימֵי בְנֵיכֶם עַל הָאֲדָמָה אֲשֶׁר נִשְׁבַּע יְיָ לַאֲבֹתֵיכֶם לָתֵת לָהֶם, כִּימֵי הַשָּׁמַיִם עַל הָאָרֶץ.

וַיֹּאמֶר יְיָ אֶל מֹשֶׁה לֵּאמֹר. דַּבֵּר אֶל בְּנֵי יִשְׂרָאֵל וְאָמַרְתָּ אֲלֵהֶם, וְעָשׂוּ לָהֶם צִיצִת עַל כַּנְפֵי בִגְדֵיהֶם לְדֹרֹתָם, וְנָתְנוּ עַל צִיצִת הַכָּנָף פְּתִיל תְּכֵלֶת. וְהָיָה לָכֶם לְצִיצִת, וּרְאִיתֶם אֹתוֹ וּזְכַרְתֶּם אֶת כָּל מִצְוֹת יְיָ, וַעֲשִׂיתֶם | אֹתָם, וְלֹא תָתוּרוּ אַחֲרֵי לְבַבְכֶם וְאַחֲרֵי עֵינֵיכֶם, אֲשֶׁר אַתֶּם זֹנִים אַחֲרֵיהֶם. לְמַעַן תִּזְכְּרוּ וַעֲשִׂיתֶם אֶת כָּל מִצְוֹתָי, וִהְיִיתֶם קְדֹשִׁים לֵאלֹהֵיכֶם. אֲנִי יְיָ אֱלֹהֵיכֶם, אֲשֶׁר הוֹצֵאתִי אֶתְכֶם מֵאֶרֶץ מִצְרַיִם, לִהְיוֹת לָכֶם לֵאלֹהִים, אֲנִי יְיָ אֱלֹהֵיכֶם אֱמֶת

*יְיָ - One of the names of God, is pronounced "Ado-noy".

English:

Listen Israel, *Ado-noy is our God, Ado-noy is One.
Blessed be the Name of His glorious kingdom forever and ever.
And you shall love Ado-noy, your God with all your heart, with all your
soul, and with all your possessions. And these words which I command
you today, shall be upon your heart. You shall teach them thoroughly
to your children. You shall discuss them when you sit in your house
and when you travel on the road, when you lie down and when you
rise. You shall bind them as a sign upon your hand, and they shall be
for a reminder between your eyes. And you shall write them upon the
doorposts of your house and upon your gateways.

And it will be, if you diligently listen to My commandments, which I
command you this day, to love Adonay your God, and to serve Him
with all of your heart and with all of your soul, I will give rain for your
land at the proper time, the early (fall) rain and the late (spring) rain,
and you will gather in your grain, and your wine and your oil. And I
will place grass in your fields for your cattle, and you will eat and be
satisfied. Beware, lest your hearts be swayed, and you turn astray and
worship alien gods and bow down to them. (If you do so), Ado-noy's
fury will flare up against you, and He will close the heavens and there
will be no rain, and the earth will not yield its produce, and you will
swiftly perish from the good land which Ado-noy gives you. Therefore,
place these words of Mine upon your heart and upon your soul, and
bind them for a sign on your hand, and they shall be for a reminder
between your eyes. And you shall teach these words to your children,
to speak of them when you sit in your house and when you travel on the
road, when you lie down and when you rise. And you shall write these
words on the doorposts of your house and on your gateways,- so that
your days and the days of your children may be prolonged on the land
which Ado-noy swore to give to your fathers, for as long as the heavens
are above the earth.

And Ado-noy spoke to Moses, saying: Speak to the children of Israel
and tell them, throughout the generations, make fringes on the corners
of your garments, and attach a blue thread on the fringe of each corner.
And it will be to you for fringes, and you will look upon them and
remember all the commandments of Ado-noy and fulfill them. And you
will not follow after your heart and after your eyes which cause you to
go astray. So that you may remember and fulfill all My commandments,
and be holy to your God. I am Ado-noy, your God who brought you out
of the land of Egypt to be your God; I, Ado-noy, am your true God.

* "ADO-NOY" is one of the names of God. Although hyphenated throughout this book, when praying, it should be pronounced without hyphenation.

Transliterated:

Shmaah Yis-ra-ael, Ado-noy Elo-hay-noo, Ado-noy Eh-chaad. Ba-rooch Shame K'vod Mal-choo-toe L'olam Va-ed.

V'ah-hav-tah eight Ado-noy Elo-he-cha, b'choel l'vav-chah, ooh-v'choel naf-sh'chah, ooh-v'choel m'oh-deh-chah. V'hah-you ha-d'vah-reem ha-ay-leh, ah-sher ah-no-cheey m'tzav-chah ha-yoem, ahl l'va-veh-chah. V-she-nan-tom l'vah-neh-chah, v'dee-bar-tah bahm, b'sheev-t'chah b'vay-teh-chah, ooh-v'lech-teh-chah vah-deh-rech, ooh-v'shach-b'chah, oohve-koo-meh-chah. Ooh-k'shar-tom l'oat ahl yah-deh-chah, v'ha-you l'toe-tah-foet bain ay-necha. Ooh-ch'tav-tom ahl m'zoo-zote Bay-te-chah ooh-vee-shar-eh-chah.

V'hah-yah eem sha-mo-ah teesh-m'oo ehl meetz-voe-tay, ah-sher ah-no-chee mee-t'zav-eh et-chem hah-yom, l'ah-ha-va eight Ado-noy El-oh-hay-chem ooh-l'avdo, b'choal l'vav-chem ooh-v'choal naf-sh'chem. V'nah-ta-tee m'tar artz-chem b'eeto, yoe-reh ooh-mal-kosh, v'ah-saf-tah d'gan-eh-cha v'tee-row-sh-chah v'yeetz-ha-re-chah. V'nah-ta-tee ay-sev b'sod-chah leev-hem-teh-chah, v'ah-chal-tah v'sah-vah-tah. He-sham-roo lah-chem pen yee'f-teh l'vav-chem, v'sar-tem v'ah-vah-d'tem Elo-heem ah-chay-reem v'heesh-ta-cha-vee-tem la-hem. V'cha-rah ahf Ado-noy ba-chem, v'ah-tzar eight ha-shah-mayeem v'low yee-yeh mah-tar, v'hah-ah-da-ma low tee-tain eht y'voo-lah, va-ah-vah'd-tem m'hay-ra may-ahl ha-aretz ha-toe-va ah-sher Ado-noy no-tain la-chem. V'sam-tem eht d'va-r'eye ay-leh ahl l'vav-chem v'ahl naf-sh-chem, ooh-kshar-tem owe-tom l'oat ahl yed-chem, v'ha-yoo l'to-ta-fot bain ay-neh-chem. V'lee-ma-d'tem owe-tom eht b'nay-chem l'dah-bear bom, b'sheev-t'cha b'vay-te-cha, ooh-v'lech-t'cha va-derech, ooh-v'shach-b'cha, ooh-v'coo-me-cha. Ooh-ch'tav-tom ahl m'zoo-zote bay-teh-cha ooh-vee-sha-re-cha. L'mon year-boo y'may-chem vee-may v'nay-chem ahl ha-ah-da-ma ah-sher nee'sh-ba Ado-noy la-ah-vo-tay-chem la-tate la-hem, kee-may ha-sha-ma-yeem ahl ha-ah-retz.

Va-yo-mer Ado-noy ehl Moshe lay-more. Dah-bear ehl b'nay Yis-ra-ael v'ah-mar-ta ah-lay-hem, v'ah-sue la-hem t'zee-tzeet ahl con-fay veeg-day-hem l'doe-roe-tom, v'not-noo ahl t'zee-tzeet ha-ka-naf p'teal t'chay-let. V'ha-ya la-chem l'tzee-tzeet, Ooh-r'ee-tem owe-toe ooh-z'char-tem eht coal meetz-vote Ado-noy, v'ah-see-tem owe-tom, v'low ta-too-roo ah-cha-ray l'vav-chem v'ah-cha-ray ay-neh-chem, ah-sher ah-tem zo-neem ah-cha-ray-hem. L'mon teez-k'roo v'ah-see-tem eht coal meetz-voe-tie, v'h'yee-tem k'do-sheem lay-lo-hay-chem. Ah-nee Ado-noy Eh-lo-hay-chem, ah-sher hoe-t'zay-tee eht-chem may-eh-retz meetz-rah-yeem, lee-oat la-chem lay-lo-heem, ah-nee Ado-noy Elo-hay-chem eh-met.

Donning the Talit

The blessing to recite when donning the Talit is:

English: *Blessed are You, Ado-nay*, our God, King of the Universe, Who has made us holy with His commandments and commanded us to wrap ourselves with tzitzit.*

Hebrew: בָּרוּךְ אַתָּה יְיָ אֱלֹהֵינוּ מֶלֶךְ הָעוֹלָם, אֲשֶׁר קִדְּשָׁנוּ בְּמִצְוֹתָיו, וְצִוָּנוּ לְהִתְעַטֵּף בַּצִיצִת

Transliterated: Baruch atta Ado-noy, Elo-hey-noo melech haolam, asher kidshanoo b'meetzvotav v'zeevanoo l'heetahtayf ba'zeezeet.

Watch a brief video demonstration of 'Donning the Talit', at SimplyJewishOnline.com/videodemonstrations.

* "ADO-NOY"- is the name of God, and throughout this book, it is hyphenated out of respect, but when you say it, it should be pronounced without hyphenation.

Tzitzit and Talit Katan

The blessing to recite when putting on Tzitzit or a Talit Katan is:

Hebrew: בָּרוּךְ אַתָּה יְיָ אֱלֹהֵינוּ מֶלֶךְ הָעוֹלָם, אֲשֶׁר קִדְּשָׁנוּ בְּמִצְוֹתָיו, וְצִוָּנוּ עַל מִצְוַת צִיצִת

English: *Blessed are You, Ado-noy, our God, King of the Universe, Who has made us holy with His commandments, and commanded us concerning the mitzvah of Tzitzit.*

Transliterated:

Ba-rooch ah-ta Ado-noy, Elo-hey-noo meh-lech ha-owe-lom, ah-sher
kid-sha-noo b'meetz-voe-tav vitz-ee-va-noo ahl meetz-vat tzee-tzeet.

Tefilin

When putting on Tefilin two blessings are recited. The first blessing is
recited when putting the Tefilin on your arm.

Hebrew: בָּרוּךְ אַתָּה יְיָ אֱלֹהֵינוּ מֶלֶךְ הָעוֹלָם, אֲשֶׁר קִדְּשָׁנוּ בְּמִצְוֹתָיו,
וְצִוָּנוּ לְהָנִיחַ תְּפִלִּין

English:
*Blessed are You, Ado-noy, our God, King of the Universe, Who has
made us holy with His commandments, and commanded us to put on
Tefilin.*

Transliterated:
Ba-rooch ah-ta Ado-noy, Elo-hey-noo meh-lech ha-owe-lom, ah-sher
kid-sha-noo b'meetz-voe-tav vitz-ee-va-noo l'hah-nee-och t'fill-in.

The second blessing is recited when putting the Tefilin on your head.

Hebrew: בָּרוּךְ אַתָּה יְיָ אֱלֹהֵינוּ מֶלֶךְ הָעוֹלָם, אֲשֶׁר קִדְּשָׁנוּ בְּמִצְוֹתָיו,
וְצִוָּנוּ עַל מִצְוַת תְּפִלִּין

English: *Blessed are You, Ado-noy, our God, King of the Universe,
Who has made us holy with His commandments, and commanded us
concerning the mitzvah of Tefilin.*

Transliterated: Ba-rooch ah-ta Ado-noy, Elo-hey-noo meh-lech
ha-owe-lom, ah-sher kid-sha-noo b'meetz-voe-tav vitz-ee-va-noo ahl
meetz-vat t'fil-in.

Immediately upon completing the second blessing say:

Hebrew: בָּרוּךְ שֵׁם כְּבוֹד מַלְכוּתוֹ לְעוֹלָם וָעֶד.

English:
Blessed be the Name of His glorious kingdom forever and ever.

Transliterated:

Ba-rooch shame k'voed mal-choo-to l'oh-lom va-ed.

While wrapping the straps around your middle finger it is traditional to say:

Hebrew:

וְאֵרַשְׂתִּיךְ לִי לְעוֹלָם, וְאֵרַשְׂתִּיךְ לִי בְּצֶדֶק וּבְמִשְׁפָּט וּבְחֶסֶד וּבְרַחֲמִים.
וְאֵרַשְׂתִּיךְ לִי בֶּאֱמוּנָה, וְיָדַעַתְּ אֶת יְיָ.

English: And I will betroth you to Me forever, and I will betroth you to Me with righteousness, in justice, in kindness, and in mercy. And I will betroth you to Me in truthfulness, and you will know Ado-noy.

Transliterated: V'ay-rahs-tee-ch lee l'oh-lom, v'ay-rahs-tee-ch lee b'tzedek ooh-v'meesh-pot ooh-v'chesed ooh-v'rah-cha-meem. v'ay-rahs-tee-ch lee b'Emoo-nah, v'ya-daat eht Ado-noy.

At the time you put up a mezuzah you say the following blessing:

Hebrew: בָּרוּךְ אַתָּה יְיָ אֱלֹהֵינוּ מֶלֶךְ הָעוֹלָם, אֲשֶׁר קִדְּשָׁנוּ בְּמִצְוֹתָיו,
וְצִוָּנוּ לִקְבֹּעַ מְזוּזָה

English:
Blessed are You Ado-noy, our God, King of the Universe, Who has made us holy with His commandments, and commanded us to affix Mezuzot.

Transliterated:
Ba-rooch ah-ta Ado-noy, Elo-hey-noo meh-lech ha-owe-lom, ah-sher kid-sha-noo b'meetz-voe-tav vitz-ee-va-noo leek-boe-ah mezuzah.

Watch a brief video demonstration of 'Putting Up a Mezuzah', at SimplyJewishOnline.com/videodemonstrations.

Simply Jewish

RESOURCE II

— The Sheva Brachot, Wedding Blessings

Hebrew:

שבע ברכות

בָּרוּךְ אַתָּה יְיָ אֱלֹהֵינוּ מֶלֶךְ הָעוֹלָם, בּוֹרֵא פְּרִי הַגָּפֶן.

בָּרוּךְ אַתָּה יְיָ אֱלֹהֵינוּ מֶלֶךְ הָעוֹלָם, שֶׁהַכֹּל בָּרָא לִכְבוֹדוֹ.

בָּרוּךְ אַתָּה יְיָ אֱלֹהֵינוּ מֶלֶךְ הָעוֹלָם, יוֹצֵר הָאָדָם.

בָּרוּךְ אַתָּה יְיָ אֱלֹהֵינוּ מֶלֶךְ הָעוֹלָם, אֲשֶׁר יָצַר אֶת הָאָדָם בְּצַלְמוֹ, בְּצֶלֶם דְּמוּת תַּבְנִיתוֹ, וְהִתְקִין לוֹ מִמֶּנּוּ בִּנְיַן עֲדֵי עַד. בָּרוּךְ אַתָּה יְיָ, יוֹצֵר הָאָדָם.

שׂוֹשׂ תָּשִׂישׂ וְתָגֵל הָעֲקָרָה, בְּקִבּוּץ בָּנֶיהָ לְתוֹכָהּ בְּשִׂמְחָה. בָּרוּךְ אַתָּה יְיָ, מְשַׂמֵּחַ צִיּוֹן בְּבָנֶיהָ.

שַׂמֵּחַ תְּשַׂמַּח רֵעִים הָאֲהוּבִים, כְּשַׂמֵּחֲךָ יְצִירְךָ בְּגַן עֵדֶן מִקֶּדֶם. בָּרוּךְ אַתָּה יְיָ, מְשַׂמֵּחַ חָתָן וְכַלָּה.

בָּרוּךְ אַתָּה יְיָ אֱלֹהֵינוּ מֶלֶךְ הָעוֹלָם, אֲשֶׁר בָּרָא שָׂשׂוֹן וְשִׂמְחָה, חָתָן וְכַלָּה, גִּילָה, רִנָּה, דִּיצָה וְחֶדְוָה, אַהֲבָה וְאַחֲוָה וְשָׁלוֹם וְרֵעוּת. מְהֵרָה, יְיָ אֱלֹהֵינוּ, יִשָּׁמַע בְּעָרֵי יְהוּדָה וּבְחֻצוֹת יְרוּשָׁלַיִם, קוֹל שָׂשׂוֹן וְקוֹל שִׂמְחָה, קוֹל חָתָן וְקוֹל כַּלָּה, קוֹל מִצְהֲלוֹת חֲתָנִים מֵחֻפָּתָם וּנְעָרִים מִמִּשְׁתֵּה נְגִינָתָם. בָּרוּךְ אַתָּה יְיָ, מְשַׂמֵּחַ חָתָן עִם הַכַּלָּה.

זימון בסעודת נשואין של(שבעת ימי משתה)
הַמְזַמֵּן נוֹטֵל כּוֹס שֶׁל יַיִן בְּיָדוֹ וְאוֹמֵר: רַבּוֹתַי, נְבָרֵךְ.
הַמְסוּבִּים עוֹנִים: יְהִי שֵׁם יְיָ מְבֹרָךְ מֵעַתָּה וְעַד עוֹלָם.
וְהַמְזַמֵּן חוֹזֵר: יְהִי שֵׁם יְיָ מְבֹרָךְ מֵעַתָּה וְעַד עוֹלָם.
דְּוַי הָסֵר וְגַם חָרוֹן, וְאָז אִלֵּם בְּשִׁיר יָרוֹן,
נְחֵנוּ בְּמַעְגְּלֵי צֶדֶק, שְׁעֵה בִּרְכַּת בְּנֵי אַהֲרֹן.
בִּרְשׁוּת מָרָנָן וְרַבָּנָן וְרַבּוֹתַי, נְבָרֵךְ אֱלֹהֵינוּ שֶׁהַשִּׂמְחָה בִּמְעוֹנוֹ וְשֶׁאָכַלְנוּ מִשֶּׁלּוֹ.
הַמְסוּבִּים עוֹנִים: בָּרוּךְ אֱלֹהֵינוּ שֶׁהַשִּׂמְחָה בִּמְעוֹנוֹ, וְשֶׁאָכַלְנוּ מִשֶּׁלּוֹ וּבְטוּבוֹ חָיִינוּ.

וְהַמְזַמֵן חוֹזֵר: בָּרוּךְ אֱלֹהֵינוּ שֶׁהַשִּׂמְחָה בִּמְעוֹנוֹ, וְשֶׁאָכַלְנוּ מִשֶּׁלּוּ וּבְטוּבוֹ חָיִינוּ. וּמברכים ברכת המזון ואחריה שבע ברכות על כוס שניה של יין.

English:

1- Blessed are You, Ado-noy, our God, King of the Universe, Creator of the fruit of the vine.

2- Blessed are You, Ado-noy, our God, King of the Universe, in Whose honor all has been created.

3- Blessed are You, Ado-noy, our God, King of the Universe, the Creator of Man.

4- Blessed are You, Ado-noy, our God, King of the Universe, Who made Man in His image and likeness, and prepared for him the means of eternal 'building'. Blessed are You, Ado-noy, the Creator of Man.

5- Let the barren city (Jerusalem) rejoice amidst the joyous reunion with her children. Blessed are You, Ado-noy, Who brings joy to Zion with her children .

6- Let the loving couple rejoice, just as Your creations rejoiced in the Garden of Eden, long ago. Blessed are You, Ado-noy, Who brings joy to the groom and bride .

7- Blessed are You, Ado-noy, our God, King of the Universe, Who has created joy and celebration, groom and bride, rejoicing, celebration, pleasure and delight, love and brotherhood, peace and friendship. Ado-noy, our God, let there soon be heard in the cities of Judea, and in the streets of Jerusalem, the sound of joy and the sound of celebration, the voice of the groom and the voice of the bride, the jubilant sounds of grooms from their wedding canopies and young men from the song-filled feasts. Blessed are You, Adonoy, Who gladdens the groom and bride.

Transliterated:

1- Ba-rooch ah-ta Ado-noy, Elo-hey-noo meh-lech ha-owe-lom, boe-ray pree Ha-gafen.

2- Ba-rooch ah-ta Ado-noy, Elo-hey-noo meh-lech ha-owe-lom, sheh-ha-coal ba-rah leech-voe-doe.

3- Ba-rooch ah-ta Ado-noy, Elo-hey-noo meh-lech ha-owe-lom, yo-sair ha-ah-dom.

4- Ba-rooch ah-ta Ado-noy, Elo-hey-noo meh-lech ha-owe-lom, ah-sher yah-sar eht ha-ah-dom, b'sal-moe, b'seh-lem d'moot tav-nee-toe, v'hees-keen low me-ma-noo been-yon ah-day odd. Ba-rooch ah-ta Ado-noy , yo-sair ha-a-dom.

5- Sow'ss ta-sees v'ta-gail ha-ak-arah, b'kee-boo'tz ba-neh-ha l'tow-chah b'seem-cha. Ba-rooch ah-ta Ado-noy, m'sa-ay-ach tzee-own b'va-ne-hah.

6- Sa-mach t'sa-mach ray-eem ha-ah-who-veem, k'sa-may-cha-cha y'sear-cha b'gone ay-den me-ka-dem. Ba-rooch ah-ta Ado-noy, m'sa-may-ach cha-tan v'cha-lah.

7- Ba-ruch ah-ta Ado-noy, Elo-hey-noo meh-lech ha-owe-lom, ah-sher ba-rah sa-son v'seem-cha, cha-tan v'cha-lah, gee-lah, ree-na, dee-t'sah v'ched-vah, aha-vah v'ach-ah-vah v'shalom v'ray-oot. M'hay-rah, Ado-noy Elo-hey-noo, yee-shama b'ah-ray Y'who-dah ooh-vchoo-soet Yeroo-sha-la-yeem, coal sa-son v'coal seem-cha, coal cha-tan v'coal ka-lah, coal meats-ha-loat cha-ta-neem may-choo-pa-tom ooh-na-reem me-me-shtay n'gee-na-tom. Ba-rooch ah-ta Ado-noy, m'sa-may-ach cha-tan eem ha-ka-lah.

RESOURCE III
— The Mourner's Kaddish

Hebrew:

יִתְגַּדַּל וְיִתְקַדַּשׁ שְׁמֵהּ רַבָּא. בְּעָלְמָא דִּי בְרָא כִרְעוּתֵהּ, וְיַמְלִיךְ מַלְכוּתֵהּ בְּחַיֵּיכוֹן וּבְיוֹמֵיכוֹן וּבְחַיֵּי דְכָל בֵּית יִשְׂרָאֵל, בַּעֲגָלָא וּבִזְמַן קָרִיב, וְאִמְרוּ אָמֵן.

יְהֵא שְׁמֵהּ רַבָּא מְבָרַךְ לְעָלַם וּלְעָלְמֵי עָלְמַיָּא.

יִתְבָּרַךְ וְיִשְׁתַּבַּח וְיִתְפָּאַר וְיִתְרוֹמַם וְיִתְנַשֵּׂא וְיִתְהַדָּר וְיִתְעַלֶּה וְיִתְהַלָּל שְׁמֵהּ דְּקֻדְשָׁא בְּרִיךְ הוּא, לְעֵלָּא מִן כָּל (בעשי"ת לְעֵלָּא וּלְעֵלָּא מִכָּל) בִּרְכָתָא וְשִׁירָתָא תֻּשְׁבְּחָתָא וְנֶחֱמָתָא, דַּאֲמִירָן בְּעָלְמָא, וְאִמְרוּ אָמֵן.

יְהֵא שְׁלָמָא רַבָּא מִן שְׁמַיָּא, וְחַיִּים)טוֹבִים(עָלֵינוּ וְעַל כָּל יִשְׂרָאֵל, וְאִמְרוּ אָמֵן.

עֹשֶׂה שָׁלוֹם בִּמְרוֹמָיו, הוּא יַעֲשֶׂה שָׁלוֹם עָלֵינוּ וְעַל כָּל יִשְׂרָאֵל, וְאִמְרוּ אָמֵן.

English:

May His great Name be exalted and sanctified. In the world that He created according to His will, may He (openly) rule His Kingdom in your days and lifetime, and in the lifetimes of the entire house of Israel, speedily, at a rapidly approaching time, and let us say, Amen.

May His great Name be blessed forever and ever.

Blessed, praised, glorified, exalted, lifted up, honored, elevated, and praised (with songs) is the Name of the Holy One, blessed be He, above all the blessings and songs, praises and consolations that we say in the world, and let us say, Amen.

May there be granted from Heaven great peace and life for us and for all Israel, and let us say, Amen.

May He, Who makes peace above, make peace for us and for all of Israel, and let us say, Amen.

Transliterated: Yeet-ga-doll v'yeet-ka-dosh shmay rah-bah.
B'ahl-mah dee v'rah cheer-oo-tay, v'yom-leech mahl-choo-tay
b'cha-yay-chown ooh-v'yo-may-chown ooh-vcha-yay d'choal bait
Yis-ra-ael, bah-gah-lah ooh-viz-mon ka-reev, v'eem-rooh Ah-main.

Y'hay shmay rah-baah m'va-roch l'oh-lom ooh-l'al-may ahl-maya.

Yeet-ba-rach v'yeesh-ta-bach v'yeet-pa-ar v'yeet-row-mom v'yeet-
na-say v'yeet-ha-dar v'yeet-ah-lay v'yeet-ha-lal shmay d'kood-sha
breeych who, l'ay-la mean coal bear-cha-ta v'shear-ah-ta two'sh-
b'cha-ta v'neh-cheh-mah-ta, d'ah-me-ran b'ahl-mah, v'eem-roo
Ah-main.

Y'hay shlah-mah rah-bah mean shma-yah, v'chaim ah-lay-noo
v'ahl coal Yis-ra-ael, v'eem-roo Ah-main.

Oh-say shalom beem-row-mav, who y'ah-say shalom ah-lay-noo
v'ahl coal Yis-ra-ael, v'eem-roo Ah-main.

RESOURCE IV
— Shabbat Blessings and Prayers

Shabbat Checklist

Time Check: Confirm candle lighting time, well in advance.

- Candle Lighting
- Shalom Alaychem
- Ayshet Chayil
- Blessing the Children
- Kiddush
- Washing Hands For Challah
- Hamotzee
- The Festive Shabbat Meal
- Zmeerot: Singing at the Shabbat Table
- D'var Torah/Sharing Words of Torah
- Grace After Meals/Birkat Hamazon/ Bentching

Shabbat (& holiday) Candle Lighting

SHABBAT:

Hebrew:

בָּרוּךְ אַתָּה יְיָ אֱלֹהֵינוּ מֶלֶךְ הָעוֹלָם, אֲשֶׁר קִדְּשָׁנוּ
בְּמִצְוֹתָיו, וְצִוָּנוּ לְהַדְלִיק נֵר שֶׁל שַׁבָּת

English: *Blessed are You, Ado-noy, our God, King of the Universe, Who has made us holy with His commandments, and commanded us to light Shabbat candles.*

Transliterated: Ba-rooch ah-ta Ado-noy, Elo-hey-noo meh-lech ha-owe-lom, ah-sher kid-sha-noo b'meetz-voe-tav vitz-ee-va-noo le'had-leek nair shel Shabbat.

HOLIDAY:

Hebrew: בָּרוּךְ אַתָּה יְיָ אֱלֹהֵינוּ מֶלֶךְ הָעוֹלָם, אֲשֶׁר קִדְּשָׁנוּ בְּמִצְוֹתָיו,
וְצִוָּנוּ לְהַדְלִיק נֵר שֶׁל יוֹם טוֹב

English: *Blessed are You, Ado-noy, our God, King of the Universe, Who has made us holy with His commandments, and commanded us to light holiday candles.*

Transliterated: Ba-rooch ah-ta Ado-noy, Elo-hey-noo meh-lech ha-owe-lom, ah-sher kid-sha-noo b'meetz-voe-tav vitz-ee-va-noo le'had-leek nair shel yoem toe'v.

The Friday Night Blessings, Including Kiddush

SHALOM ALAYCHEM

Hebrew:

שָׁלוֹם עֲלֵיכֶם, מַלְאֲכֵי הַשָּׁרֵת, מַלְאֲכֵי עֶלְיוֹן, מִמֶּלֶךְ מַלְכֵי הַמְּלָכִים,
הַקָּדוֹשׁ בָּרוּךְ הוּא.
בּוֹאֲכֶם לְשָׁלוֹם, מַלְאֲכֵי הַשָּׁלוֹם, מַלְאֲכֵי עֶלְיוֹן, מִמֶּלֶךְ מַלְכֵי הַמְּלָכִים,
הַקָּדוֹשׁ בָּרוּךְ הוּא.
בָּרְכוּנִי לְשָׁלוֹם, מַלְאֲכֵי הַשָּׁלוֹם, מַלְאֲכֵי עֶלְיוֹן, מִמֶּלֶךְ מַלְכֵי הַמְּלָכִים,
הַקָּדוֹשׁ בָּרוּךְ הוּא.
צֵאתְכֶם לְשָׁלוֹם, מַלְאֲכֵי הַשָּׁלוֹם, מַלְאֲכֵי עֶלְיוֹן, מִמֶּלֶךְ מַלְכֵי הַמְּלָכִים,
הַקָּדוֹשׁ בָּרוּךְ הוּא.

English:

Welcome, ministering angels, messengers of the Most High, of the King of Kings, the Holy One, Blessed be He.
Come in peace, angels of peace, messengers of the Most High, of the King of Kings, the Holy one, Blessed be He.
Bless me with peace, angels of peace, messengers of the Most High, of the King of Kings, the Holy one, Blessed be He.
Go in peace, angels of peace, messengers of the Most High, of the King of Kings, the Holy one, Blessed be He.

Transliterated:

Shalom ah-lay-chem, ma-la-chay ha-sha-rate, ma-la-chay El-y'own, me-meh-lech mal-chay ha-m'la-cheem, ha-ka-dosh ba-rooch who.

Bo-ah-chem l'shalom, ma-la-chay ha-shalom, ma-la-chay El-y'own, me-meh-lech mal-chay ha-m'la-cheem, ha-ka-dosh ba-rooch who.

Bar-choo-nee l'shalom, mal-a-chay ha-sha-lom, mal-a-chay El-y'own, me-meh-lech mal-chay ha-m'la-cheem, ha-ka-dosh ba-rooch who.

Tsayt-'chem l'shalom, mal-a-chay ha-sha-lom, mal-a-chay El-y'own, me-meh-lech mal-chay ha-m'la-cheem, ha-ka-dosh ba-rooch who.

Ayshet Chayil - A Woman Of Valor

Hebrew:

אֵשֶׁת חַיִל מִי יִמְצָא, וְרָחֹק מִפְּנִינִים מִכְרָהּ. בָּטַח בָּהּ לֵב בַּעְלָהּ, וְשָׁלָל לֹא יֶחְסָר. גְּמָלַתְהוּ טוֹב וְלֹא רָע, כֹּל יְמֵי חַיֶּיהָ. דָּרְשָׁה צֶמֶר וּפִשְׁתִּים, וַתַּעַשׂ בְּחֵפֶץ כַּפֶּיהָ. הָיְתָה כָּאֳנִיּוֹת סוֹחֵר, מִמֶּרְחָק תָּבִיא לַחְמָהּ. וַתָּקָם בְּעוֹד לַיְלָה, וַתִּתֵּן טֶרֶף לְבֵיתָהּ, וְחֹק לְנַעֲרֹתֶיהָ. זָמְמָה שָׂדֶה וַתִּקָּחֵהוּ, מִפְּרִי כַפֶּיהָ נָטְעָה כָּרֶם. חָגְרָה בְעוֹז מָתְנֶיהָ, וַתְּאַמֵּץ זְרוֹעֹתֶיהָ. טָעֲמָה כִּי טוֹב סַחְרָהּ, לֹא יִכְבֶּה בַלַּיְלָה נֵרָהּ. יָדֶיהָ שִׁלְּחָה בַכִּישׁוֹר, וְכַפֶּיהָ תָּמְכוּ פָלֶךְ. כַּפָּהּ פָּרְשָׂה לֶעָנִי, וְיָדֶיהָ שִׁלְּחָה לָאֶבְיוֹן. לֹא תִירָא לְבֵיתָהּ מִשָּׁלֶג, כִּי כָל בֵּיתָהּ לָבֻשׁ שָׁנִים. מַרְבַדִּים עָשְׂתָה לָּהּ, שֵׁשׁ וְאַרְגָּמָן לְבוּשָׁהּ. נוֹדָע בַּשְּׁעָרִים בַּעְלָהּ, בְּשִׁבְתּוֹ עִם זִקְנֵי אָרֶץ. סָדִין עָשְׂתָה וַתִּמְכֹּר, וַחֲגוֹר נָתְנָה לַכְּנַעֲנִי. עֹז וְהָדָר לְבוּשָׁהּ, וַתִּשְׂחַק לְיוֹם אַחֲרוֹן. פִּיהָ פָּתְחָה בְחָכְמָה, וְתוֹרַת חֶסֶד עַל לְשׁוֹנָהּ. צוֹפִיָּה הֲלִיכוֹת בֵּיתָהּ, וְלֶחֶם עַצְלוּת לֹא תֹאכֵל. קָמוּ בָנֶיהָ וַיְאַשְּׁרוּהָ, בַּעְלָהּ וַיְהַלְלָהּ. רַבּוֹת בָּנוֹת עָשׂוּ חָיִל, וְאַתְּ עָלִית עַל כֻּלָּנָה. שֶׁקֶר הַחֵן וְהֶבֶל הַיֹּפִי, אִשָּׁה יִרְאַת יְיָ הִיא תִתְהַלָּל. תְּנוּ לָהּ מִפְּרִי יָדֶיהָ, וִיהַלְלוּהָ בַשְּׁעָרִים מַעֲשֶׂיהָ.

English:

A WOMAN OF VALOR, who can find? She is more precious than corals. Her husband places his trust in her, to his benefit. She brings him good, not bad, all the days of her life. She finds wool and flax and happily does her handiwork. She is like the merchant ships, bringing food from far away. She awakes while it is still night to provide food for her household, and a fair portion for her maid. She plans and then carries out her plan, she purchases a field and with the fruit of her labor she plants a vineyard. She strengthens herself, making her arms powerful. She knows that her trade is profitable. Her light does not go out at night. She stretches out her hands to the staff and her palms hold the spindle. She opens her hand to the poor and reaches her hands out to the needy. Her household has no fear of the snow because they are clothed in fine linen clothing. She makes her own accessories and wears fine linen clothing. Her husband is known at the (Town) gates, where he sits with the Elders of the land. She makes and sells linens, and provides sashes to the merchants. She is robed in strength and dignity and smiles upon contemplating the future. Her mouth opens with wisdom and words of kindness are always on her tongue. She looks after the dealings of her household and never tastes the bread of laziness. Her children arise and please her. Her husband praises her, telling her, "Many women have excelled, but you outshine them all.". Grace is elusive and beauty is vain, but a woman who is God fearing, she shall be praised. Credit her for the fruit of her labor and let her achievements praise her at the gate.

Transliterated:

Ay-shet cha-y'eel mee-yeem-tza, v'ra-choek mee-pnee-neem meech-ra. Bah-tach bah lay've ba-la, v'sha-lal low yech-sar. G'ma-la-too toe'v v'low rah, coal y'may cha-ye-hah, dar-sha tze-mer ooh-feesh-team, vah-tas b'chay-fetz ka-peh-hah. Hi-tah ka-ah-nee-yot sow-chair, me-mer-chak ta-vee lach-ma, vah-tokem be-ode lie-lah, vah-tee-ten teh-ref l'vay-ta v'choek l'nay-row-te-hah. Za-m'ma sah-deh va-tee-ka-chey-hoo, me-pree chah-pee-ha nah-ta ka-rem. Chag-rah v'oz mat-neh-hah, va-ta-metz z'row-te-hah. Tah-ma key toe'v sach-ra, low yeech-beh ba-lay-lah nay-ra, ya-de-ha sheil-cha va-key-shore, v'cha-peh-hah tom-choo fa-lech. Ka-pah par-sah leh-ah-nee, v'ya-deh-ha sheel-cha l'ev-yown. Low tee-rah l'vay-tah me-sha-leg, key chol vay-tah la-vush sha-neem.

Mar-va-deem ah-sta-la, shaish v'ar-ga-man l'voo-sha, noe-da ba-sh'ah-reem ba'la, b'sheave-toe eem zeek-nay ah-retz. Sah-deen ahs-ta va-teem-core, va-cha-gor not-nah la-kna-nee. Oz v'ha-dar l'voo-sha, va-tees-chak l'yoem ah-cha-rown. Pee-hah pot-cha v'chuch-ma, v'toe-rot cheh-sed ahl l'show-na, tzo-fee-ya ha-lee-chot bay-ta, v'le-chem ahtz-loot low toe-chail. Ka-moo va-ne-hah v'yash-roo-hah, ba-lah va-y'ha-le-lah, ra-boat ba-note ah-soo cha-yeel, v'aht ah-leet ahl coo-la-na. Sheh-ker ha-chain, v'heh-vel ha-yo-fee, ee-shah yee-rot

Ado-noy, hee teet-ha-lal. T'noo lah, me-pree yah-deh-ha, vee-ha-leh-loo-hah ba-sh-ah-reem mah-seh-ha.

Blessing the Children

Hebrew:

The blessing for a daughter: יְשִׂמֵךְ אֱלֹהִים כְּשָׂרָה רִבְקָה רָחֵל וְלֵאָה

The blessing for a son: יְשִׂמְךָ אֱלֹהִים כְּאֶפְרַיִם וְכִמְנַשֶּׁה.

Conclude for both daughters and sons:

יְבָרֶכְךָ יְיָ וְיִשְׁמְרֶךָ. יָאֵר יְיָ פָּנָיו אֵלֶיךָ וִיחֻנֶּךָּ.
יִשָּׂא יְיָ פָּנָיו אֵלֶיךָ וְיָשֵׂם לְךָ שָׁלוֹם.

English:

The blessing for a daughter:
May God make you like Sarah, Rebecca, Rachel and Leah.

The blessing for a son:
May God make you like Ephraim and Menashe.

Conclude for both daughters and sons:
May God bless you and protect you.
May God shine His face towards you and show you favor.
May God be favorably disposed towards you and grant you peace.

Transliterated:

For a daughter:
Y'seem-cha Elo-heem k'Sarah, Reeve-kah, Rah-ch'ail, v'Lay-ah.

For a son:
Y'seem-cha Elo-heem k'Ef-rah-yeem ooh-M'na-sheh

Conclude for daughters and sons:
Y'va-rech-eh-cha Ado-noy v'yeesh-m'reh-chah,
Ya-air Ado-noy pah-nav ay-leh-cha vee-choo-neh-chah,
Yee-sah Ado-noy pah-nav ay-le-cha v'yah-sem l'chah sha-lom.

Kiddush

Hebrew:

וַיְהִי עֶרֶב וַיְהִי בֹקֶר יוֹם הַשִּׁשִׁי. וַיְכֻלּוּ הַשָּׁמַיִם וְהָאָרֶץ וְכָל צְבָאָם. וַיְכַל אֱלֹהִים בַּיּוֹם הַשְּׁבִיעִי מְלַאכְתּוֹ אֲשֶׁר עָשָׂה, וַיִּשְׁבֹּת בַּיּוֹם הַשְּׁבִיעִי, מִכָּל מְלַאכְתּוֹ אֲשֶׁר עָשָׂה, וַיְבָרֶךְ אֱלֹהִים אֶת יוֹם הַשְּׁבִיעִי וַיְקַדֵּשׁ אֹתוֹ, כִּי בוֹ שָׁבַת מִכָּל מְלַאכְתּוֹ, אֲשֶׁר בָּרָא אֱלֹהִים לַעֲשׂוֹת.

סַבְרִי מָרָנָן וְרַבָּנָן וְרַבּוֹתַי:
בָּרוּךְ אַתָּה יְיָ אֱלֹהֵינוּ מֶלֶךְ הָעוֹלָם, בּוֹרֵא פְּרִי הַגָּפֶן.

בָּרוּךְ אַתָּה יְיָ אֱלֹהֵינוּ מֶלֶךְ הָעוֹלָם, אֲשֶׁר קִדְּשָׁנוּ בְּמִצְוֹתָיו וְרָצָה בָנוּ, וְשַׁבַּת קָדְשׁוֹ בְּאַהֲבָה וּבְרָצוֹן הִנְחִילָנוּ זִכָּרוֹן לְמַעֲשֵׂה בְרֵאשִׁית, כִּי הוּא יוֹם תְּחִלָּה לְמִקְרָאֵי קֹדֶשׁ, זֵכֶר לִיצִיאַת מִצְרָיִם, כִּי בָנוּ בָחַרְתָּ וְאוֹתָנוּ קִדַּשְׁתָּ מִכָּל הָעַמִּים, וְשַׁבַּת קָדְשְׁךָ בְּאַהֲבָה וּבְרָצוֹן הִנְחַלְתָּנוּ. בָּרוּךְ אַתָּה יְיָ, מְקַדֵּשׁ הַשַּׁבָּת.

English:

IT WAS EVENING, then morning of the sixth day and the Heaven and earth were completed, and all their hosts. And on the seventh day God completed the work He had been doing. And God blessed the seventh day and made it holy because on it God ceased His work of creating. Blessed are You, Ado-noy, King of the Universe, Creator of the fruit of the vine.

Blessed are You, Ado-noy, King of the Universe, Who made us holy with His commandments and favored us by giving us His holy Sabbath with love and favor as our heritage, as a reminder of Creation. It is the foremost day of the holy days marking the Exodus from Egypt. Because of all the nations, You chose us and made us holy and You gave us Your holy Sabbath, out of love and favor, as our heritage. Blessed are You, Ado-noy, who sanctifies the Sabbath.

Transliterated:

Va-y'hee eh-rev, va-y'hee voe-ker yoem ha-shee-she, va-y'choo-loo ha-sha-ma-yeem v'ha-ah-retz, v'choel tz'va-am. Va-y'chal Elo-heem ba-yoem ha-shvee-ee m'lach-toe ah-sher ah-sah, va-yeesh-boat ba-yoem ha-shvee-ee, mee-coal m'lach-toe ah-sher ah-sah. Va-y'vah-rech Elo-heem eht yoem ha-shvee-ee vah-yee-kah-daish oh-toe, key voe sha-vat mee-coal m'lach-toe ah-sher bah-rah Elo-heem la-ah-sow't.

Sav-ree mah-ra-non v'rah-bah-nan v'rob-oh-tie:
Ba-rooch ah-tah Ado-noy, Elo-hey-noo meh-lech ha-owe-lom, boe-ray pree ha-ga-fen. Ba-rooch ah-ta Ado-noy, Elo-hey-noo meh-lech ha-oe-lom, ah-sher kid-shanoo b'meetz-voe-tav v'rah-sah va-noo, v'Shah-bat kod-show, b'ah-ha-vah ooh-v'rah-sown heen-chee-lah-noo zee-ka-r'own l'ma-ah-say v'ray-sheet, key who yoem t'chee-lah l'meek-ray koe-desh, zay-cher l'yitz-ee-aht meetz-rah-yeem, key va-noo v'char-tah v'oe-ta-noo key-dash-tah mee-coal hah-ah-meem, v'sha-bat kad-sheh-chah b'ah-hah-vah ooh-rah-tzon heen-chal -tah-noo. Ba-rooch ah-tah Ado-noy, m'kah-daish ha-Shabbat.

Washing Hands

Hebrew: בָּרוּךְ אַתָּה יְיָ, אֱלֹהֵינוּ מֶלֶךְ הָעוֹלָם, אֲשֶׁר קִדְּשָׁנוּ בְּמִצְוֹתָיו, וְצִוָּנוּ עַל נְטִילַת יָדַיִם

English: *Blessed are You, Ado-noy, our God, King of the Universe, Who has made us holy with His commandments, and commanded us regarding washing hands.*

Transliterated: Ba-rooch ah-ta Ado-noy, Elo-hey-noo meh-lech ha-owe-lom, ah-sher kid-sha-noo b'meetz-voe-tav vitz-ee-va-noo ahl n'tee-lot yah-dah-yeem.

Watch a brief video demonstration of 'Washing for Bread/Challah', at SimplyJewishOnline.com/videodemonstrations.

Hamotzee: The Blessing for Bread & Challah

Hebrew: בָּרוּךְ אַתָּה יְיָ, אֱלֹהֵינוּ מֶלֶךְ הָעוֹלָם, הַמּוֹצִיא לֶחֶם מִן הָאָרֶץ.

English: *Blessed are You, Ado-noy, our God, King of the Universe, Who brings forth bread from the earth.*

Transliterated: Ba-rooch ah-ta Ado-noy, Elo-hey-noo meh-lech ha-owe-lom, ha-mo-tzee leh-chem mean ha-ah-retz.

Birkat Hamazon / Grace-After-Meals

Hebrew:

בָּרוּךְ אַתָּה יְיָ, אֱלֹהֵינוּ מֶלֶךְ הָעוֹלָם, הַזָּן אֶת הָעוֹלָם כֻּלּוֹ בְּטוּבוֹ בְּחֵן בְּחֶסֶד וּבְרַחֲמִים, הוּא נוֹתֵן לֶחֶם לְכָל בָּשָׂר כִּי לְעוֹלָם חַסְדּוֹ. וּבְטוּבוֹ הַגָּדוֹל תָּמִיד לֹא חָסַר לָנוּ, וְאַל יֶחְסַר לָנוּ מָזוֹן לְעוֹלָם וָעֶד. בַּעֲבוּר שְׁמוֹ הַגָּדוֹל, כִּי הוּא אֵל זָן וּמְפַרְנֵס לַכֹּל וּמֵטִיב לַכֹּל, וּמֵכִין מָזוֹן לְכָל בְּרִיּוֹתָיו אֲשֶׁר בָּרָא. בָּרוּךְ אַתָּה יְיָ, הַזָּן אֶת הַכֹּל.

נוֹדֶה לְךָ, יְיָ אֱלֹהֵינוּ, עַל שֶׁהִנְחַלְתָּ לַאֲבוֹתֵינוּ אֶרֶץ חֶמְדָּה טוֹבָה וּרְחָבָה, וְעַל שֶׁהוֹצֵאתָנוּ, יְיָ אֱלֹהֵינוּ, מֵאֶרֶץ מִצְרַיִם, וּפְדִיתָנוּ מִבֵּית עֲבָדִים, וְעַל בְּרִיתְךָ שֶׁחָתַמְתָּ בִּבְשָׂרֵנוּ, וְעַל תּוֹרָתְךָ שֶׁלִּמַּדְתָּנוּ, וְעַל חֻקֶּיךָ שֶׁהוֹדַעְתָּנוּ, וְעַל חַיִּים חֵן וָחֶסֶד שֶׁחוֹנַנְתָּנוּ, וְעַל אֲכִילַת מָזוֹן שָׁאַתָּה זָן וּמְפַרְנֵס אוֹתָנוּ תָּמִיד, בְּכָל יוֹם וּבְכָל עֵת וּבְכָל שָׁעָה.

(לַחֲנֻכָּה וּפוּרִים:)
עַל הַנִּסִּים, וְעַל הַפֻּרְקָן, וְעַל הַגְּבוּרוֹת, וְעַל הַתְּשׁוּעוֹת, וְעַל הַמִּלְחָמוֹת, שֶׁעָשִׂיתָ לַאֲבוֹתֵינוּ בַּיָּמִים הָהֵם בַּזְּמַן הַזֶּה.

לַחֲנֻכָּה:
בִּימֵי מַתִּתְיָהוּ בֶּן יוֹחָנָן כֹּהֵן גָּדוֹל, חַשְׁמוֹנַאי וּבָנָיו, כְּשֶׁעָמְדָה מַלְכוּת יָוָן הָרְשָׁעָה עַל עַמְּךָ יִשְׂרָאֵל לְהַשְׁכִּיחָם תּוֹרָתֶךָ, וּלְהַעֲבִירָם מֵחֻקֵּי רְצוֹנֶךָ, וְאַתָּה בְּרַחֲמֶיךָ הָרַבִּים עָמַדְתָּ לָהֶם בְּעֵת צָרָתָם, רַבְתָּ אֶת רִיבָם, דַּנְתָּ אֶת דִּינָם, נָקַמְתָּ אֶת נִקְמָתָם, מָסַרְתָּ גִבּוֹרִים בְּיַד חַלָּשִׁים, וְרַבִּים בְּיַד מְעַטִּים, וּטְמֵאִים בְּיַד טְהוֹרִים, וּרְשָׁעִים בְּיַד צַדִּיקִים, וְזֵדִים בְּיַד עוֹסְקֵי תוֹרָתֶךָ. וּלְךָ עָשִׂיתָ שֵׁם גָּדוֹל וְקָדוֹשׁ בְּעוֹלָמֶךָ, וּלְעַמְּךָ יִשְׂרָאֵל עָשִׂיתָ תְּשׁוּעָה גְדוֹלָה וּפֻרְקָן כְּהַיּוֹם הַזֶּה. וְאַחַר כֵּן בָּאוּ בָנֶיךָ לִדְבִיר בֵּיתֶךָ, וּפִנּוּ אֶת הֵיכָלֶךָ, וְטִהֲרוּ אֶת מִקְדָּשֶׁךָ, וְהִדְלִיקוּ נֵרוֹת בְּחַצְרוֹת קָדְשֶׁךָ, וְקָבְעוּ שְׁמוֹנַת יְמֵי חֲנֻכָּה אֵלּוּ, לְהוֹדוֹת וּלְהַלֵּל לְשִׁמְךָ הַגָּדוֹל.

לְפוּרִים:
בִּימֵי מָרְדְּכַי וְאֶסְתֵּר בְּשׁוּשַׁן הַבִּירָה, כְּשֶׁעָמַד עֲלֵיהֶם הָמָן הָרָשָׁע, בִּקֵּשׁ לְהַשְׁמִיד לַהֲרֹג וּלְאַבֵּד אֶת כָּל הַיְּהוּדִים, מִנַּעַר וְעַד זָקֵן, טַף וְנָשִׁים, בְּיוֹם אֶחָד, בִּשְׁלוֹשָׁה עָשָׂר לְחֹדֶשׁ שְׁנֵים עָשָׂר, הוּא חֹדֶשׁ אֲדָר, וּשְׁלָלָם לָבוֹז. וְאַתָּה בְּרַחֲמֶיךָ הָרַבִּים הֵפַרְתָּ אֶת עֲצָתוֹ, וְקִלְקַלְתָּ אֶת מַחֲשַׁבְתּוֹ, וַהֲשֵׁבוֹתָ לּוֹ גְּמוּלוֹ בְּרֹאשׁוֹ, וְתָלוּ אוֹתוֹ וְאֶת בָּנָיו עַל הָעֵץ.)

וְעַל הַכֹּל, יְיָ אֱלֹהֵינוּ, אֲנַחְנוּ מוֹדִים לָךְ, וּמְבָרְכִים אוֹתָךְ, יִתְבָּרַךְ שִׁמְךָ
בְּפִי כָּל חַי תָּמִיד לְעוֹלָם וָעֶד. כַּכָּתוּב, וְאָכַלְתָּ וְשָׂבָעְתָּ, וּבֵרַכְתָּ אֶת יְיָ
אֱלֹהֶיךָ עַל הָאָרֶץ הַטֹּבָה אֲשֶׁר נָתַן לָךְ. בָּרוּךְ אַתָּה יְיָ, עַל הָאָרֶץ וְעַל
הַמָּזוֹן.

רַחֵם, יְיָ אֱלֹהֵינוּ, עַל יִשְׂרָאֵל עַמֶּךָ, וְעַל יְרוּשָׁלַיִם עִירֶךָ, וְעַל צִיּוֹן מִשְׁכַּן
כְּבוֹדֶךָ, וְעַל מַלְכוּת בֵּית דָּוִד מְשִׁיחֶךָ, וְעַל הַבַּיִת הַגָּדוֹל וְהַקָּדוֹשׁ
שֶׁנִּקְרָא שִׁמְךָ עָלָיו. אֱלֹהֵינוּ, אָבִינוּ, רְעֵנוּ, זוּנֵנוּ, פַּרְנְסֵנוּ, וְכַלְכְּלֵנוּ,
וְהַרְוִיחֵנוּ, וְהַרְוַח לָנוּ יְיָ אֱלֹהֵינוּ מְהֵרָה מִכָּל צָרוֹתֵינוּ, וְנָא אַל תַּצְרִיכֵנוּ,
יְיָ אֱלֹהֵינוּ, לֹא לִידֵי מַתְּנַת בָּשָׂר וָדָם, וְלֹא לִידֵי הַלְוָאָתָם, כִּי אִם לְיָדְךָ
הַמְּלֵאָה, הַפְּתוּחָה, הַקְּדוֹשָׁה וְהָרְחָבָה, שֶׁלֹּא נֵבוֹשׁ וְלֹא נִכָּלֵם לְעוֹלָם
וָעֶד.

לשבת

רְצֵה וְהַחֲלִיצֵנוּ יְיָ אֱלֹהֵינוּ בְּמִצְוֹתֶיךָ וּבְמִצְוַת יוֹם הַשְּׁבִיעִי הַשַּׁבָּת
הַגָּדוֹל וְהַקָּדוֹשׁ הַזֶּה. כִּי יוֹם זֶה גָּדוֹל וְקָדוֹשׁ הוּא לְפָנֶיךָ, לִשְׁבָּת בּוֹ
וְלָנוּחַ בּוֹ בְּאַהֲבָה כְּמִצְוַת רְצוֹנֶךָ, וּבִרְצוֹנְךָ הָנִיחַ לָנוּ יְיָ אֱלֹהֵינוּ, שֶׁלֹּא
תְהֵא צָרָה וְיָגוֹן וַאֲנָחָה בְּיוֹם מְנוּחָתֵנוּ. וְהַרְאֵנוּ יְיָ אֱלֹהֵינוּ בְּנֶחָמַת צִיּוֹן
עִירֶךָ, וּבְבִנְיַן יְרוּשָׁלַיִם עִיר קָדְשֶׁךָ, כִּי אַתָּה הוּא בַּעַל הַיְשׁוּעוֹת וּבַעַל
הַנֶּחָמוֹת.

בר"ח ויו"ט וחול המועד וראש השנה

אֱלֹהֵינוּ וֵאלֹהֵי אֲבוֹתֵינוּ, יַעֲלֶה וְיָבֹא, וְיַגִּיעַ, וְיֵרָאֶה, וְיֵרָצֶה, וְיִשָּׁמַע,
וְיִפָּקֵד, וְיִזָּכֵר זִכְרוֹנֵנוּ וּפִקְדוֹנֵנוּ, דָּוִד עַבְדֶּךָ, וְזִכְרוֹן יְרוּשָׁלַיִם עִיר קָדְשֶׁךָ,
לְפָנֶיךָ, לִפְלֵיטָה, לְטוֹבָה, לְחֵן וּלְחֶסֶד וּלְרַחֲמִים, וְזִכְרוֹן אֲבוֹתֵינוּ, וְזִכְרוֹן מָשִׁיחַ בֶּן
וְזִכְרוֹן כָּל עַמְּךָ בֵּית יִשְׂרָאֵל לְפָנֶיךָ, לִפְלֵיטָה, לְטוֹבָה, לְחֵן וּלְחֶסֶד וּלְרַחֲמִים, לְחַיִּים וּלְשָׁלוֹם, בְּיוֹם

רֹאשׁ הַחֹדֶשׁ ו חַג הַמַּצּוֹת ו חַג הַשָּׁבֻעוֹת ו חַג הַסֻּכּוֹת ו
הַשְּׁמִינִי חַג הָעֲצֶרֶת ו הַזִּכָּרוֹן

הַזֶּה. זָכְרֵנוּ, יְיָ אֱלֹהֵינוּ, בּוֹ לְטוֹבָה, וּפָקְדֵנוּ בוֹ לִבְרָכָה, וְהוֹשִׁיעֵנוּ בוֹ
לְחַיִּים. וּבִדְבַר יְשׁוּעָה וְרַחֲמִים, חוּס וְחָנֵּנוּ, וְרַחֵם עָלֵינוּ וְהוֹשִׁיעֵנוּ, כִּי
אֵלֶיךָ עֵינֵינוּ, כִּי אֵל מֶלֶךְ חַנּוּן וְרַחוּם אָתָּה.

וּבְנֵה יְרוּשָׁלַיִם עִיר הַקֹּדֶשׁ בִּמְהֵרָה בְיָמֵינוּ. בָּרוּךְ אַתָּה יְיָ, בּוֹנֵה בְרַחֲמָיו
יְרוּשָׁלָיִם. אָמֵן.

בָּרוּךְ אַתָּה יְיָ אֱלֹהֵינוּ מֶלֶךְ הָעוֹלָם, הָאֵל, אָבִינוּ, מַלְכֵּנוּ, אַדִּירֵנוּ,
בּוֹרְאֵנוּ, גּוֹאֲלֵנוּ, יוֹצְרֵנוּ, קְדוֹשֵׁנוּ קְדוֹשׁ יַעֲקֹב, רוֹעֵנוּ רוֹעֵה יִשְׂרָאֵל,
הַמֶּלֶךְ הַטּוֹב וְהַמֵּטִיב לַכֹּל, שֶׁבְּכָל יוֹם וָיוֹם הוּא הֵטִיב, הוּא מֵטִיב,
נֶחָמָה, הוּא יֵיטִיב לָנוּ. הוּא גְמָלָנוּ, הוּא גוֹמְלֵנוּ, הוּא יִגְמְלֵנוּ לָעַד, לְחֵן
וּלְחֶסֶד וּלְרַחֲמִים וּלְרֶוַח הַצָּלָה וְהַצְלָחָה, בְּרָכָה וִישׁוּעָה,
פַּרְנָסָה וְכַלְכָּלָה, וְרַחֲמִים וְחַיִּים וְשָׁלוֹם וְכָל טוֹב, וּמִכָּל טוּב לְעוֹלָם אַל
יְחַסְּרֵנוּ.

הָרַחֲמָן, הוּא יִמְלוֹךְ עָלֵינוּ לְעוֹלָם וָעֶד.

הָרַחֲמָן, הוּא יִתְבָּרַךְ בַּשָּׁמַיִם וּבָאָרֶץ.

הָרַחֲמָן, הוּא יִשְׁתַּבַּח לְדוֹר דּוֹרִים, וְיִתְפָּאַר בָּנוּ לָעַד וּלְנֵצַח נְצָחִים,
וְיִתְהַדַּר בָּנוּ לָעַד וּלְעוֹלְמֵי עוֹלָמִים.

הָרַחֲמָן, הוּא יְפַרְנְסֵנוּ בְּכָבוֹד.

הָרַחֲמָן, הוּא יִשְׁבּוֹר עֻלֵּנוּ מֵעַל צַוָּארֵנוּ וְהוּא יוֹלִיכֵנוּ קוֹמְמִיּוּת לְאַרְצֵנוּ.

הָרַחֲמָן, הוּא יִשְׁלַח לָנוּ בְּרָכָה מְרֻבָּה בַּבַּיִת הַזֶּה, וְעַל שֻׁלְחָן זֶה
שֶׁאָכַלְנוּ עָלָיו.

הָרַחֲמָן, הוּא יִשְׁלַח לָנוּ אֶת אֵלִיָּהוּ הַנָּבִיא זָכוּר לַטּוֹב, וִיבַשֶּׂר לָנוּ
בְּשׂוֹרוֹת טוֹבוֹת יְשׁוּעוֹת וְנֶחָמוֹת.

הָרַחֲמָן, הוּא יְבָרֵךְ אֶת (אָבִי מוֹרִי) בַּעַל הַבַּיִת הַזֶּה, וְאֶת (אִמִּי מוֹרָתִי)
בַּעֲלַת הַבַּיִת הַזֶּה, אוֹתָם וְאֶת בֵּיתָם וְאֶת זַרְעָם וְאֶת כָּל אֲשֶׁר לָהֶם,

הָרַחֲמָן, הוּא יְבָרֵךְ אוֹתִי (וְאָבִי / וְאִמִּי / וְאִשְׁתִּי /וְזַרְעִי / וְאֶת כָּל אֲשֶׁר
לִי)

אוֹתָנוּ וְאֶת כָּל אֲשֶׁר לָנוּ, כְּמוֹ שֶׁנִּתְבָּרְכוּ אֲבוֹתֵינוּ, אַבְרָהָם יִצְחָק
וְיַעֲקֹב, בַּכֹּל, מִכֹּל, כֹּל, כֵּן יְבָרֵךְ אוֹתָנוּ כֻּלָּנוּ יַחַד בִּבְרָכָה שְׁלֵמָה, וְנֹאמַר
אָמֵן.

בַּמָּרוֹם יְלַמְּדוּ עֲלֵיהֶם וְעָלֵינוּ זְכוּת, שֶׁתְּהֵא לְמִשְׁמֶרֶת שָׁלוֹם, וְנִשָּׂא
בְרָכָה מֵאֵת יְיָ, וּצְדָקָה מֵאֱלֹהֵי יִשְׁעֵנוּ, וְנִמְצָא חֵן וְשֵׂכֶל טוֹב בְּעֵינֵי
אֱלֹהִים וְאָדָם.

לשבת הָרַחֲמָן, הוּא יַנְחִילֵנוּ יוֹם שֶׁכֻּלּוֹ שַׁבָּת וּמְנוּחָה לְחַיֵּי הָעוֹלָמִים.
לר"ח הָרַחֲמָן, הוּא יְחַדֵּשׁ עָלֵינוּ אֶת הַחֹדֶשׁ הַזֶּה לְטוֹבָה וְלִבְרָכָה.
ליום טוב הָרַחֲמָן, הוּא יַנְחִילֵנוּ יוֹם שֶׁכֻּלּוֹ טוֹב.
לר"ה הָרַחֲמָן, הוּא יְחַדֵּשׁ עָלֵינוּ אֶת הַשָּׁנָה הַזֹּאת לְטוֹבָה וְלִבְרָכָה.
לסוכות הָרַחֲמָן, הוּא יָקִים לָנוּ אֶת סֻכַּת דָּוִד הַנּוֹפָלֶת.

הָרַחֲמָן, הוּא יְזַכֵּנוּ לִימוֹת הַמָּשִׁיחַ וּלְחַיֵּי הָעוֹלָם הַבָּא.
בְּחֹל מַגְדִּיל (**בשבת ור"ח ויו"ט וחול המועד וראש השנה** מִגְדּוֹל)
יְשׁוּעוֹת מַלְכּוֹ, וְעֹשֶׂה חֶסֶד לִמְשִׁיחוֹ לְדָוִד וּלְזַרְעוֹ עַד עוֹלָם. עֹשֶׂה שָׁלוֹם
בִּמְרוֹמָיו, הוּא יַעֲשֶׂה שָׁלוֹם עָלֵינוּ וְעַל כָּל יִשְׂרָאֵל, וְאִמְרוּ אָמֵן.

יְראוּ אֶת יְיָ קְדֹשָׁיו, כִּי אֵין מַחְסוֹר לִירֵאָיו. כְּפִירִים רָשׁוּ וְרָעֵבוּ, וְדֹרְשֵׁי
יְיָ לֹא יַחְסְרוּ כָל טוֹב. הוֹדוּ לַיְיָ כִּי טוֹב, כִּי לְעוֹלָם חַסְדּוֹ. פּוֹתֵחַ
אֶת יָדֶךָ, וּמַשְׂבִּיעַ לְכָל חַי רָצוֹן. בָּרוּךְ הַגֶּבֶר אֲשֶׁר יִבְטַח בַּיְיָ, וְהָיָה יְיָ
מִבְטַחוֹ. נַעַר הָיִיתִי גַם זָקַנְתִּי, וְלֹא רָאִיתִי צַדִּיק נֶעֱזָב, וְזַרְעוֹ מְבַקֶּשׁ
לָחֶם. יְיָ עֹז לְעַמּוֹ יִתֵּן, יְיָ יְבָרֵךְ אֶת עַמּוֹ בַשָּׁלוֹם.

English:

Blessed are You, Ado-noy, Our God, King of the Universe, Who provides food for the entire world in His goodness, with grace, kindness, and mercy. He supplies sustenance (literally 'bread') for all living beings, for His kindness is everlasting.

And because of His great goodness, we have never lacked, nor will we ever lack sustenance. For the sake of His great Name, because He is God who feeds and sustains all, and is good to all, and Who supplies food for all the creatures He created. Blessed are You, Ado-noy, Who provides food for all.

We thank You, Ado-noy, our God, for giving to our fathers as an inheritance, a desirable, good and spacious land; and Ado-noy, our God, for bringing us out of Egypt, and rescuing us from slavery; and for Your covenant which You sealed in our flesh; and for Your Torah which You taught us; and for Your laws which You have revealed to us; and for the life, grace and kindness You have granted us; and for the food which You supply and provide for us constantly, every day, all the time, and at every hour.

(On Chanukah and Purim) *add the following: We thank You for the miracles, for the redemption, for the mighty actions, for the salvation, and for the wars that You fought for our fathers in those days, during this season:*

(On Chanukah) *In the days of Matityahoo, the son of Yochannan, the High Priest, the Hasmonean, and his sons, when the evil Greek Kingdom stood up against Your nation, Israel, attempting to cause them to forget Your Torah, and to abandon the statutes that reflect Your will. You, with Your great mercy, stood by them in their time of pain. You fought their fights, and judged their disputes. You avenged them. You delivered the mighty into the hands of the weak; the many into the hands of the few; the impure into the hands of the pure; the wicked into the hands of the righteous; the wanton sinners into the hands of those immersed in Your Torah. You caused Your name to become great and sanctified in Your world. And for Your people, Israel, you brought a great salvation and redemption (like) on this day. Afterwards, Your* *sons entered the most Holy part of Your House, cleaned it, and purified the sanctuary, and lit candles in the Courtyard of the sanctuary, and established these eight days of Chanukah to thank and praise Your great Name.*

(On Purim) In the days of Mordechai and Esther, in Shushan, the capital, when the evil Haman stood up against (the Jewish nation), seeking to destroy, kill, and obliterate all Jews, young and old, the toddlers, and women, in one day, the thirteenth day of the twelfth month, which is the month of Adar, and to take their wealth as booty. You, with Your great mercy, caused his advice to be abandoned and his plans to be spurned, and brought his evil onto his own head, and they hung him and his sons on the gallows.

Ado-noy, our God, we thank You, and bless You, for everything. May Your name be blessed by the mouths of all the living, constantly, forever. As it is written, "And when you eat, and are satisfied, you shall bless Ado-noy, your God for the good land He gave you." Blessed are You, Ado-noy, for the land and for the food.

Ado-noy our God, have mercy on Israel, Your people, on Jerusalem,Your city, on Zion the dwelling place of your honor, on the kingdom of the house of David, Your anointed one, and on the great and holy house which is called by Your name. Our God, our Father, look after us, provide for us, give us a livelihood, sustain us, and provide a respite for us, a respite Ado-noy, our God, quickly, from all our troubles. Ado-noy, our God, may we never be dependent on the gifts of men or on loans, but only on Your hand, which is full, open, holy and generous, so that we never be embarrassed or shamed.

(Add On Shabbat) May it please You, Ado-noy, our God, to strengthen us through Your commandments, and the commandment of the seventh day, this great and holy Shabbat. For this day is a great and holy day before You; (we) lovingly rest on it as You commanded. And may it please You, Ado-noy, our God, to grant us relief, without any pain, or sorrow, or unhappiness on our day of rest. And show us, Ado-noy, our God, the comforting of Zion, Your city, and the rebuilding of Jerusalem, Your holy city, for You are the Lord of redemption, and the Lord of consolation.

(Add On holidays or Rosh Chodesh) Our God, and the God of our fathers, may (our prayers) ascend and reach before You, and may they be desired, heard, counted and remembered. Remember us and our fathers, remember the Messiah, the son of David, Your servant, remember Jerusalem, Your holy city, and remember all of Your people, Israel for survival, for goodness, for favor, for mercy, for life and for peace, on this: (make the appropriate selection): [holiday of Matzot], [holiday of Shavuot], [holiday of Sukkot], [holiday of Shmini Atzeret], [Day of Rememberance, (on Rosh Hashanah)], [Rosh Chodesh, (new month)]. Ado-noy, our God, remember us, this day for goodness, and blessing and deliver us for life. And as deliverance is mentioned, have mercy, spare us, favor us and deliver us. For our eyes are on You, the Almighty, gracious and merciful King).

Rebuild Jerusalem, the holy city, speedily in our days. Blessed are You, Ado-noy, Who in His mercy rebuilds Jerusalem. Amen.

Blessed are You, Ado-noy, our God, King of the Universe, the Almighty, Who is our Father, our King, our Mighty One, our Creator, our Redeemer, our Maker, our Holy One, the Holy One of Jacob, our Shepherd, the Shepherd of Israel, the King Who is good and does good to all. Each and every day He has done good, does good, and will do good to us. He gave us, He gives us, and will always give us, with grace, kindness, and mercy. He gives us respite, deliverance, success, blessing, salvation, consolation, a livelihood, nourishment, mercy, life and peace and all good things. May He never let us lack anything.
May the Merciful One rule over us forever.
May the Merciful One be blessed in heaven and on earth.
May the Merciful One be praised for all generations, and may He be glorified and honored through us forever.
May the Merciful One grant us an honorable livelihood.
May the Merciful One break the yoke from our neck and lead us upright to our land.
May the Merciful One send abundant blessing to this house and upon this table at which we have eaten.
May the Merciful One send us Elijah the prophet, who is remembered for good, who will bring us good tidings, salvation and consolation. (Select as appropriate:)

(when eating at your own table:) May the Merciful One bless me, my [wife/husband],
and my children, and all that is mine,
(when eating at parent's table:) May the Merciful One bless my father, my teacher, the man of this household, and my mother, my teacher, the lady of this household, them, and their household, their children, and all that is theirs.

(when you are a guest:) May the Merciful One bless the host and hostess, them, their children, and all that is theirs.

Just as our forefathers Abraham, Isaac, and Jacob were blessed in "all things", "from everything", and "with everything", so May He bless us, ours, and all that is ours, all of us together, with a complete blessing, and let us say, Amen.

May our pleas be heard on high, and may they serve as a merit to safeguard peace for them and for us. May we receive a blessing from Ado-noy, and righteousness from the God of our salvation. May we find favor and understanding in the sight of God and man.

(Add as appropriate:)
(On Shabbat add) *May the Merciful One cause us to inherit the day that will be a complete Shabbat and eternal rest day.*
(On holidays add) *May the Merciful One cause us to inherit the day that will be completely good.*
(On Rosh Chodesh add) *May the Merciful One make this new month a month of goodness and blessing for us.*
(On Rosh Hashanah add) *May the Merciful One make this new year a year of goodness and blessing for us.*
(On Sukkot add) *May the Merciful One build for us David's fallen Sukkah.*

May the Merciful One make us worthy of the days of the Messiah, and the life of the world to come. (God) brings about great victories for His king, and shows kindness to His anointed, to David, and to His descendants forever. May He, who makes peace above, make peace for us and for all of Israel, and let us say, Amen.

Be in awe of Ado-noy, His holy ones, for those that awe Him lack nothing. Young lions may want and hunger, but those who seek Ado-noy will not lack any good thing.

Give thanks to Ado-noy, for He is good, for His kindness is eternal. You open Your hand and satisfy the desire of all living beings.
Blessed is the man who trusts in Ado-noy, and then Ado-noy will be his security. I was young and now I am old, and yet I never seen a righteous man forsaken, with his children begging for bread. May Ado-noy give strength to His people. May Ado-noy bless His people with peace.

Transliterated:

Bah-rooch ah-ta Ado-noy, Elo-hey-noo meh-lech ha-owe-lom, ha-zahn eht ha-owe-lom coo-low b'two-voe b'chain b'cheh-said ooh-v'rah-cha-meem, who no-tain leh-chem l'choel ba-sar, key l'owe-lom chas-doe, oohv-too-voe ha-ga-dole, tah-meed low cha-sar la-noo, v'ahl yech-saar la-noo ma-zone l'owe-lom va-ed. Bah-ah-voor shmoe ha-ga-dole, key who Ail zahn ooh-m'far-nays la-coal ooh-may-teeve la-coal, ooh-may-cheen ma-zone l'choal bree-oh-tav ah-sher ba-rah. Ba-rooch ah-ta Ado-noy, ha-zahn eht ha-coal.
No-deh l'chah Ado-noy Elo-hay-noo, ahl sheh-heen-chal-tah la-ah-voe-tay-noo, eh-retz chem-dah toe-vah ooh'r-chah-vah, v'ahl sheh-hoe-tzee-tah-noo Ado-noy Elo-hay-noo, may-eh-retz meetz-rah-yeem, oof'dee-tah-noo mee-bait ah-va-deem, v'ahl breet-cha sheh-chah-tom-tah beev-sah-ray-noo, v'ahl Toe-rawt-cha sheh-lee-mahd-ta-noo, v'ahl choo-keh-cha sheh-hoe-da-ta-noo, v'ahl cha-yeem chain v'cheh-sed sheh-cho-nan-ta-noo, v'ahl ah-chee-lot ma-zone sheh-ah-tah zahn, ooh-m'far-nays oh-ta-noo tah-meed, b'choal yoem ooh-v'choal eight ooh-v'choal shah-ah.

(Add On Chanukah and Purim) Ahl ha-nee-seem, v'ahl ha-poor-con, v'ahl ha-g'voo-rote, v'ahl ha-t'shoo-oat, v'ahl ha-meal-cha-moat, sheh-ah-see-tah la-ah-voe-tay-noo bah-yah-meem ha-haim ba-zman ha-zeh.
(On Chanukah) Bee-may Ma-teet-ya-hoo ben Yo-cha-nan ko-hain ga-dole, chash-moe-noy ooh-va-nav, k'sheh-ahm-da mahl-choot Ya-vohn ha-ra-sha ahl ahm-cha Yis-rah-ael l'hash-key-chom toe-ra-teh-

cha, ooh-l'ha-ah-vee-rom may-choo-kay r'sow-ne-cha, v'ah-ta b'ra-cha-meh-cha ha-ra-beem ah-mad-tah la-hem b'eight tza-ra-tom, rav-ta eht ree-vom, don-ta eht dee-nom, na-kam-ta eht neek-ma-tom, ma-sar-ta gee-boe-reem b'yad cha-la-sheem, v'ra-beem b'yad m'ah-teem, ooh-t'may-eem b'yad t'hoe-reem, ooh-r'shah-eem b'yad tza-dee-keem, v'zay-deem b'yad oh-s'kay toe-ra-te-cha. Ooh-l'cha ah-see-ta shame ga-dole v'ka-doe'sh b'oh-la-me-chah, ooh-l'am-cha Yis-ra-ael ah-see-ta t'shoo-ah g'doe-la ooh-for-con k'ha-yoem ha-zeh. V'ah-char cain ba-ooh ba-ne-cha leed-veer bay-te-cha, ooh-fee-noo eht hay-cha-le-cha, v'tee-ha-roo eht meek-da-sheh-cha, v'heed-lee-koo nay-roet b'chatz-rote kad-sheh-cha, v'ka-voo shmoe-nat y'may cha-noo-kah ay-lew, l'hoe-dote ooh-l'ha-lail l'sheem-cha ha-ga-dol.

(On Purim) Bee-may Mord-eh-chay v'Es-ter b'shoo-shan ha-bee-rah, k'sheh-ah-mod ah-lay-hem Ha-mahn ha-rah-sha, bee-kay'sh l'hash-meed la-ha-rouge ooh-l'ah-bade eht coal ha-Y'hoo-deem, me-naar v'ad za-cain, tahf v'na-sheem, b'yoem eh-chad, beesh-low-shah ah-sar l'choe-desh shnaim ah-sar, who choe-desh ah-dar, ooh-shla-lom la-voez. V'ah-ta brah-cha-mecha ha-ra-beem hay-far-ta eht ah-tza-toe, v'keel-kal-ta eht ma-cha-shav-toe, va-ha-shay-voe-ta low g'moo-low b'row-show, v'ta-lew oh-toe v'eht ba-nov ahl ha-aytz.)

V'ahl ha-coal Ado-noy Elo-hay-noo, ah-nach-noo moe-deem lah'ch ooh-m'var-cheem oh-tach, yit-ba-rach Sheem-cha b'fee coal chai tah-mead l'owe-lom va-ed. Ka-ka-toov, v'ah-chal-ta v'sah-vah-ta, ooh-vay-rahch-ta eht Ado-noy Elo-he-cha ahl ha-ah-retz ha-toe-vah ah-sher na-ton lah'ch. Ba-rooch ah-tah Ado-noy, ahl ha-ah-retz v'ahl ha ma-zone.

Ra-chaim (nah) Ado-noy Elo-hay-noo ahl Yis-ra-ael ah-meh-cha, v'ahl Y'roo-sha-la-yeem ee-reh-cha, v'ahyl tzee-own meesh-con k'vo-de-chah, v'ahl mahl-choot bait Da-veed m'shee-che-cha, v'ahl ha-ba-yeat ha-ga-dole v'ha-ka-dosh sheh-neek-ra shim-cha ah-lahv. Elo-hay-noo ah-vee-noo r'ay-noo, zoo-nay-noo, par-n'say-noo, v'choel-clay-noo, v'har-vee-chay-noo, v'har-vach la-noo Ado-noy Elo-hay-noo m'hay-rah mee-coal tzar-oh-tay-noo, V'nah ahl tatz-ree-chay-noo, Ado-noy Elo-hay-noo, low lee-day mot-not ba-sar va-dom, v'low lee-day halva-tom, key eem l'yod-cha ha-m'lay-ah ha-p'too-cha ha-k'doe-shah v'har-cha-va, sheh-low nay-voesh v'low nee-ka-lame l'oh-lom va-ed.

(On Shabbat) R'tsay v'ha-cha-lee-tzay-noo Ado-noy Elo-hay-noo b'meetz-voe-te-cha, ooh'vmeetz-vat yoem ha-shvee-ee ha-Sha-bat ha-ga-dole v'ha-ka-dosh ha-zeh. Kee yoem zeh ga-dole v'ka-dosh who l'fa-ne-cha, leesh-boat boe v'la-noo-ach boe b'ah-ha-vah k'meetz-vot r'tzoe-neh-cha, Ooh-veer-tzown-cha ha-nee-ach la-noo Ado-noy Elo-hay-noo, sheh-low t'hay tza-rah v'ya-goen va-ah-na-chah b'yoem m'noo-cha-tay-noo. V'ha-ray-noo Ado-noy Elo-hay-noo b'neh-cha-mat tzee-own ee-reh-cha ooh-v'veen-yon Yeroo-sha-la-yeem ear kod-sheh-cha, key ah-tah who baal ha-yeh-shoo-oat ooh-vaal ha-neh-cha-moat.

(On holidays) Elo-hay-noo vay-lo-hay avoe-tay-noo, ya-leh, v'ya-voh, v'ya-gee-ah, v'yee-ra-eh, v'yea-rah-tzeh, v'yee-shah-ma, v'yee-pa-caid, v'yee-za-chair, zeech-row-nay-noo, ooh-feeg-doe-nay-noo, v'zeech-r'own avoe-tay-noo, v'zeech-r'own ma-she-ach ben Da-veed av-de-cha, v-zeech-r'own Y'roo-sha-la-yeem ear kad-sheh-cha, v'zeech-r'own coal ahm-cha bait Yis-ra-ael l'fa-ne-cha, leef-lay-ta l'toe-va l'chain ooh-l'che-said ooh-l'ra-cha-meem, l'cha-yeem ooh-l'sha-lom b'yoem:
(select as appropriate:) **(On Rosh Chodesh/New Month: Roe'sh choe-desh ha-zeh), (On Passover: Chog ha-ma-tzoet ha-zeh), (On Shavuot: Chog ha-sha-voo-oat ha-zeh), (On Rosh Hashanah: ha-zee-ka-r'own ha-zeh), (On Succot: chog ha-sue-coat ha-zeh), (On Shmini Atzeret/Simchat Torah: ha-shmee-nee chog ha-ah-tzer-et ha-zeh).**
Zach-ray-noo Ado-noy Elo-hay-noo boe L'toe-vah, ooh-fahk-day-noo voe leeve-rah-cha, v'hoe-shee-ay-noo voe l'cha-yeem, ooh-dvar y'shoe-ah v'rah-chah-meem, choos v'cha-nay-noo v'rah-ch'aim ah-lay-noo v'hoe-shee-ay-noo, key ay-leh-cha ay-neh-noo, key Ail Cha-noon v'rah-choom ah-tah.

Ooh-v'nay Yeru-sha-lah-yeem ear ha-koe-desh beem-hay-rah v'yah-may-noo. Ba-rooch ah-tah Ado-noy, boe-nay v'rah-chah-mav Yeru-sha-lah-yeem. Ah-main.

Ba-rooch ah-tah Ado-noy, Elo-hay-noo meh-lech ha-oe-lom, ha-Ail ah-vee-noo mahl-kay-noo ah-dee-ray-noo boe-ray-noo go-ah-lay-noo yotz-ray-noo k'doe-shay-noo k'doesh Ya-cove, Roe-ay-noo roe-ay Yis-rah-ael ha-meh-lech ha-toe'v v'ha-may-teev la-coal, sheh-b'choal yoem va-yoem, who hay-teev, who may-teev who yay-teev lah-noo. Who g'ma-la-noo, who goem-lay-noo, who yeeg-m'lay-noo lah-ahd, l'chain ooh-l'cheh-sed ooh-l'rah-chah-meem ooh-l'reh-vach hah-tzah-lah v'hatz-lah-chah, b'rah-cha vee-shoe-ah neh-chah-ma par-na-sa v'chal-ka-lah. V'rah-cha-meem v'chah-yeem v'shah-loem v'choel toe'v, ooh-me-coal too've l'oe-lom ahl y'chas-ray-noo.

Ha-rah-cha-mon who yeem-loe'ch ah-lay-noo l'oh-lom va-ed. Ha-rah-cha-mon who yeet-ba-rach ba-sha-ma-yeem ooh-va-ah-retz. Ha-rah-cha-mon who yeesh-ta-bach l'door doe-reem, v'yeet-pa-ar ba-noo la-odd ooh-l'nay-sach n'tza-cheem, v'yeet-ha-dar ba-noo la-odd ooh-l'oe-lay oe-la-meem. Ha-rah-cha-mon who y'far-n'say-noo b'cha-voed. Ha-rah-cha-mon who yeesh-bore ah-lay-noo may-ahl tza-va-ray-noo, v'who yoe-lee-chay-noo koe-m'me-oot l'artz-ay-noo. Ha-rah-cha-mon who yeesh-loch la-noo b'ra-chah m'roo-bah ba-ba-yeet ha-zeh, v'ahl shul-chan zeh sheh-ah-chal-noo ah-lav. Ha-ra-cha-mon who yeesh-lach la-noo eht Ei-ya-hoo ha-na-vee za-chur la-toe'v, vee-va-ser la-noo b'sow-r'oat toe-vote y'shoe-oat v'neh-cha-moat.

Ha-rah-cha-mon who y'va-raych....(add as appropriate):
(when eating at your parents' table:)...eht ah-vee moe-ree baal ha-ba-yeet, v'eht eemee moe-ra-tee ba-lot ha-ba-yeet ha-zeh, oh-tom v'eht bay-tom v'eht za-rom v'eht coal ah-sher la-hem.
(for one's hosts:)...eht baal ha-ba-yeet ha-zeh, v'eht ba-lot ha-ba-yeet ha-zeh, oh-tom v'eht bay-tom v'eht coal ah-sher la-hem.
(when eating at home:)...oh-tee v'eht (eesh-tee, husband for wife) (ba-lee, wife for husband), v'eht za-ree v'eht coal ah-sher lee.

All continue: v'eht coal ha-m'sue-been con, oh-ta-noo v'eht coal ah-sher la-noo, k'moe sheh-neet-bar-choo ah-voe-tay-noo Av-ra-ham Yitz-chak v'Yah-cove ba-coal mee-coal coal, cane y'va-raych oh-tanoo coo-la-noo ya-chad, beeve-ra-chah shlay-mah, v'no-mar ah-main.

Ba-ma-rome y'lam-doo ah-lay-hem v'ah-lay-noo z'choot sheh-t'hay l'meesh-meh-ret sha-lom. V'nee-sah v'ra-chah may-eight Ado-noy, ooh-tzda-kah may-Elo-hay yee-shay-noo, V'neem-tza chain v'say-chel toe'v b'ay-nay Elo-heem v'ah-dom.

Add as Approprate:
(On Shabbat) Ha-rah-cha-mon who yon-chee-lay-noo yoem sheh-coo-low Shabbat ooh-meh'new-cha l'cha-yea ha-oh-la-meem.
(On holidays) Ha-rah-cha-mon who yon-chee-lay-noo yoem sheh-coo-low toe'v.
(On Rosh Chodesh) Ha-rah-cha-mon who y'cha-daish ah-lay-noo eht ha-cho-desh ha-zeh l'toe-vah v'leeve-brah-cha.
(On Rosh Hashanah) Ha-rah-cha-mon who y'cha-daish ah-lay-noo eht ha-sha-nah- ha-zoet l'toe-vah v'leeve-brah-cha.
(On Sukkot) Ha-rah-cha-mon who yah-keem la-noo eht sue-cot Da-veed ha-no-fall-et.

Ha-rah-cha-mon who y'za-kay-noo lee-mote ha-moe-she-ach, ooh-l'cha-yay ha-oe-lom ha-bah. Meeg-dole y'shoe-oat mahl-coe, v'oh-seh cheh-sed leem-she-choe, l'Da-veed ooh-l'za-roe odd oh-lahm. Oh-seh shalom beem-row-mov, who yah-seh shalom ah-lay-noo v'ahl coal Yis-ra-ael, v'eem-roo ah-main.

Y'roo eht Ado-noy k'doe-shav, key ain mach-soar lee-ray-ov. Kfee-reem ra-shoe, v'ra-ay-voo, v'door-shay Ado-noy low yach-se-roo chol toe'v. Hoe-doo la-Ado-noy key toe'v, key l'oh-lom chas-doe, poe-tay-ach eht yah-deh-cha, ooh-mas-bee-ah l'chol chai rah-tzon. Ba-rooch ha-geh-ver ah-sher yeev-toch ba'Ado-noy, v'ha-yah Ado-noy meeve-tah-cho. Na'ar ha-yee-tee gom za-kan-tee, v'low ra-ee-tee tza-deek ne-eh-zav, v'za-roe m'va-kaish la-chem. Ado-noy oz l'ah-moe yee-tain, Ado-noy y'va-raych eht ah-moe va-shalom.

Morning Kiddush for Shabbat & holidays

Hebrew:

בשבת: וְשָׁמְרוּ בְנֵי יִשְׂרָאֵל אֶת הַשַּׁבָּת, לַעֲשׂוֹת אֶת הַשַּׁבָּת לְדֹרֹתָם בְּרִית עוֹלָם. בֵּינִי וּבֵין בְּנֵי יִשְׂרָאֵל אוֹת הִיא לְעֹלָם, כִּי שֵׁשֶׁת יָמִים עָשָׂה יְיָ אֶת הַשָּׁמַיִם וְאֶת הָאָרֶץ, וּבַיּוֹם הַשְּׁבִיעִי שָׁבַת וַיִּנָּפַשׁ.

זָכוֹר אֶת יוֹם הַשַּׁבָּת לְקַדְּשׁוֹ. שֵׁשֶׁת יָמִים תַּעֲבֹד וְעָשִׂיתָ כָּל מְלַאכְתֶּךָ. וְיוֹם הַשְּׁבִיעִי שַׁבָּת לַיְיָ אֱלֹהֶיךָ, לֹא תַעֲשֶׂה כָל מְלָאכָה, אַתָּה וּבִנְךָ וּבִתֶּךָ עַבְדְּךָ וַאֲמָתְךָ וּבְהֶמְתֶּךָ, וְגֵרְךָ אֲשֶׁר בִּשְׁעָרֶיךָ. כִּי שֵׁשֶׁת יָמִים עָשָׂה יְיָ אֶת הַשָּׁמַיִם וְאֶת הָאָרֶץ אֶת הַיָּם וְאֶת כָּל אֲשֶׁר בָּם, וַיָּנַח הַשְּׁבִיעִי –

עַל כֵּן בֵּרַךְ יְיָ אֶת יוֹם הַשַּׁבָּת וַיְקַדְּשֵׁהוּ.

בשלש רגלים:
אֵלֶּה מוֹעֲדֵי יְיָ מִקְרָאֵי קֹדֶשׁ, אֲשֶׁר תִּקְרְאוּ אֹתָם בְּמוֹעֲדָם.
וַיְדַבֵּר מֹשֶׁה אֶת מֹעֲדֵי יְיָ, אֶל בְּנֵי יִשְׂרָאֵל.

בראש השנה:
תִּקְעוּ בַחֹדֶשׁ שׁוֹפָר, בַּכֶּסֶה לְיוֹם חַגֵּנוּ. כִּי חֹק לְיִשְׂרָאֵל הוּא, מִשְׁפָּט לֵאלֹהֵי יַעֲקֹב.

סַבְרִי מָרָנָן וְרַבָּנָן וְרַבּוֹתַי:
בָּרוּךְ אַתָּה יְיָ אֱלֹהֵינוּ מֶלֶךְ הָעוֹלָם, בּוֹרֵא פְּרִי הַגָּפֶן.

(בסוכות: בָּרוּךְ אַתָּה יְיָ אֱלֹהֵינוּ מֶלֶךְ הָעוֹלָם, אֲשֶׁר קִדְּשָׁנוּ בְּמִצְוֹתָיו, וְצִוָּנוּ לֵישֵׁב בַּסֻּכָּה.)

English:

On Shabbat:

And the Children of Israel shall keep the Sabbath, observing the Sabbath as an everlasting covenant throughout the generations. It is a sign between Me and the Children of Israel for all time that the Lord created the heavens and the earth in six days and on the seventh day He finished and rested, (Exodus 31:16).

Remember the Sabbath and keep it holy. Six days you shall labor and do all your work, but the seventh day is the Sabbath for the Lord your God. You may not do any work, neither you, nor your son or daughter, male or female worker, cattle, or stranger who is in your gates. Because in six days the Lord created the Heavens, the earth, the sea, and all they contain, and He rested on the seventh day. Therefore, the Lord blessed the Shabbat and made it holy, (Exodus 20:8).

Blessed are You, Ado-noy, our God, King of the Universe, Who brings forth the fruit of the vine.

(On holidays) *These are the festivals of Ado-noy, holy gatherings, which are to be proclaimed at the appointed times. And Moses spoke to the Children of Israel, designating the festivals. Blessed are You, Ado-noy, our God, King of the Universe, Who brings forth the fruit of the vine.*

(On Rosh Hashanah) *Blow the Shofar in that month, at the full moon of our festive day. It is a statute of Israel, an ordinance of the God of Jacob. Blessed are You, Ado-noy, our God, King of the Universe, Who brings forth the fruit of the vine.*

(On Sukkot, when in the Sukkah add…) *Blessed are You, Ado-noy, our God, King of the Universe, Who sanctified us with His commandments and commanded us to dwell in the Sukkah.*

Transliterated:

(On Shabbat) V'shom-roo v'nay Yisrael eht ha-Sha-bat, la-ah-sow't eht ha-Sha-bat l'doe-roe-tom breet owe-lom. Bay-nee ooh-vain b'nay Yisrael oat he l'oh-lom, key shay-shet ya-meem ah-sah Ado-noy eht ha-sha-ma-yeem v'eht ha-aretz, ooh-va-yoem ha-shvee-ee sha-vat va-yee-na-fash.

Za-chor eht yoem ha-sha-bat l'kod-show. Shay-shet ya-meem ta-ah-voad v'ah-see-tah coal m'lahch-te-cha. V'yoem ha-shvee-ee Sha-bat la-Ado-noy Elo-heh-cha, low ta-ah-seh choal m'la-cha, ah-ta ooh-veen-cha ooh-vee-te-cha av-d'cha va-amat-cha ooh-vhem-t'cha, v'gair-cha ah-sher bee-shar-eh-cha. Key shay-shet ya-meem ah-sah Ado-noy eht ha-sha-ma-yeem v'eht ha-ah-retz eht ha-yoem v'eht coal ah-sher bam, va-ya-nach ba-yoem ha-shvee-ee.
Ahl cain bay-rach Ado-noy eht yoem ha-Sha-bat va-y'kod-shay-who.

Sav-ree mah-ra-nan v'rah-bah-ban v'rob-oh-tie:
Ba-rooch ah-tah Ado-noy, Elo-hey-noo meh-lech ha-owe-lom, boe-ray pree ha-ga-fen.

(On holidays) Ay-leh moe-ah-day Ado-noy meek-ra-ay koe-desh ah-sher teek-roo oh-tom b'moe-ah-dom. Va-y'da-bear Moe-sheh eht moe-ah-day Ado-noy ehl b'nay Yis-ra-ael. Sav-ree mah-ra-nan v'rah-bah-nan v'rob-oh-tie. Ba-rooch ah-tah Ado-noy, Elo-hey-noo meh-lech ha-owe-lom, boe-ray pree ha-ga-fen.

(On Rosh Hashanah) Teek-oo va-choe-desh show-far, ba-key-seh l'yoem cha-gay-noo. Key choek l'Yis-ra-ael who meesh-pot lay-lo-hay Ya-cove. Sav-ree mah-ra-nan v'rah-bah-ban v'rob-oh-tie. Ba-rooch ah-tah Ado-noy, Elo-hey-noo meh-lech ha-owe-lom, boe-ray pree ha-ga-fen.

(On Sukkot, when in the Sukkah add...) Ba-rooch ah-ta Ado-noy, Elo-hey-noo meh-lech ha-owe-lom, ah-sher kid-sha-noo b'meetz-voe-tav vitz-ee-va-noo lay-shave ba-sue-kah.

Havdalah

Hebrew:

סדר הבדלה

הִנֵּה אֵל יְשׁוּעָתִי, אֶבְטַח וְלֹא אֶפְחָד, כִּי עָזִּי וְזִמְרָת יָה יְיָ, וַיְהִי לִי לִישׁוּעָה. וּשְׁאַבְתֶּם מַיִם בְּשָׂשׂוֹן, מִמַּעַיְנֵי הַיְשׁוּעָה. לַיְיָ הַיְשׁוּעָה, עַל עַמְּךָ בִרְכָתֶךָ סֶּלָה. יְיָ צְבָאוֹת עִמָּנוּ, מִשְׂגָּב לָנוּ אֱלֹהֵי יַעֲקֹב סֶלָה. יְיָ צְבָאוֹת, אַשְׁרֵי אָדָם בֹּטֵחַ בָּךְ. יְיָ הוֹשִׁיעָה, הַמֶּלֶךְ יַעֲנֵנוּ בְיוֹם קָרְאֵנוּ. לַיְהוּדִים הָיְתָה אוֹרָה וְשִׂמְחָה וְשָׂשׂוֹן וִיקָר. כֵּן תִּהְיֶה לָנוּ. כּוֹס יְשׁוּעוֹת אֶשָּׂא, וּבְשֵׁם יְיָ אֶקְרָא.

סַבְרִי מָרָנָן וְרַבָּנָן וְרַבּוֹתַי:
בָּרוּךְ אַתָּה יְיָ, אֱלֹהֵינוּ מֶלֶךְ הָעוֹלָם, בּוֹרֵא פְּרִי הַגָּפֶן.
בָּרוּךְ אַתָּה יְיָ, אֱלֹהֵינוּ מֶלֶךְ הָעוֹלָם, בּוֹרֵא מִינֵי בְשָׂמִים.
בָּרוּךְ אַתָּה יְיָ, אֱלֹהֵינוּ מֶלֶךְ הָעוֹלָם, בּוֹרֵא מְאוֹרֵי הָאֵשׁ.
בָּרוּךְ אַתָּה יְיָ, אֱלֹהֵינוּ מֶלֶךְ הָעוֹלָם, הַמַּבְדִּיל בֵּין קֹדֶשׁ לְחוֹל, בֵּין אוֹר לְחֹשֶׁךְ, בֵּין יִשְׂרָאֵל לָעַמִּים, בֵּין יוֹם הַשְּׁבִיעִי לְשֵׁשֶׁת יְמֵי הַמַּעֲשֶׂה. בָּרוּךְ אַתָּה יְיָ, הַמַּבְדִּיל בֵּין קֹדֶשׁ לְחוֹל.

English:

Behold. God is my salvation; I will trust in God and not be afraid
because my strength and my song is God. And you shall draw water
with Joy from the springs of salvation, for salvation belongs to the

Lord. May Your blessings be upon Your people. The Lord is with us, the God of Jacob is our protector. Lord, happy is the man who trusts in You. Lord, save us, and answer us on the day we call. "Their was light and joy, gladness and honor for the Jewish people", (Book of Esther), so may it be for us. I will lift the cup of salvation and call on the name of the Lord.

Blessed are You, Ado-noy, our God, King of the Universe, Who brings forth the fruit of the vine.

Blessed are You, Ado-noy, our God, King of the Universe, Creator of various kinds of spices.

Blessed are You, Ado-noy, our God, King of the Universe , Creator of the lights of fire.

Blessed are You, Ado-noy, our God, King of the Universe, Who distinguishes between holy and the mundane, between light and darkness, between Israel and other nations, between the seventh day and the six working days, Blessed are You Ado-noy, who distinguishes between the holy and the mundane.

Transliterated: Hee-nay Ail y'shoo-ah-tee ev-tach v'-low ef-chad, kee ah-zee v'zeem-rot Yah Ado-noy, va-y'hee lee lee-shoo-ah. Ooh-shav-tem ma-yeem b'sa-soen me-moy-nay ha-y'shoo-ah. L'Ado-noy ha-y'shoo-ah, ahl am-chah veer-cha-te-cha seh-lah. Ado-noy tz'va-oat ee-ma-noo, mees-gov la-noo Elo-hay Ya-cove seh-lah. Ado-noy tz'va-oat ah'sh-ray ah-dam boe-tay-ach bach. Ado-noy hoe-shee-ah, ha-meh-lech ya-nay-noo b'yoem koe-ray-noo. La-Y'who-deem hi-ta oh-rah v'seem-cha, v'sa-soen vee-car, cain tee-yeh la-noo. Coe's y'shoo-oat eh-sa ooh-v'shaim Ado-noy ek-ra. Sav-ree mah-ra-nan v'rah-bah-nan v'rob-oh-tie.

Ba-rooch ah-tah Ado-noy, Elo-hey-noo meh-lech ha-owe-lom, boe-ray pree ha-ga-fen.

Ba-rooch ah-tah Ado-noy, Elo-hey-noo meh-lech ha-owe-lom, boe-ray mee-nay v'sah-meem.

Ba-rooch ah-tah Ado-noy, Elo-hey-noo meh-lech ha-owe-lom, boe-ray m'oh-ray ha-aish.

Ba-rooch ah-tah Ado-noy, Elo-hey-noo meh-lech ha-owe-lom, ha-mav-deal bain ko-desh l'chol, bain ore l'choe-shech, bain Yis-ra-ael la-ah-meem, bain yoem ha-shvee-ee l'shay-shet y'may ha-ma-ah-seh. Ba-rooch ah-ta Ado-noy, ha-mav-deal bain koe-desh l'choel.

RESOURCE V
Holiday Blessings & Prayers

Kiddush on Rosh Hashanah

Hebrew:

(בשבת: וַיְהִי עֶרֶב וַיְהִי בְקֶר

יוֹם הַשִּׁשִׁי. וַיְכֻלּוּ הַשָּׁמַיִם וְהָאָרֶץ וְכָל צְבָאָם. וַיְכַל אֱלֹהִים בַּיּוֹם הַשְּׁבִיעִי מְלַאכְתּוֹ אֲשֶׁר עָשָׂה, וַיִּשְׁבֹּת בַּיּוֹם הַשְּׁבִיעִי, מִכָּל מְלַאכְתּוֹ אֲשֶׁר עָשָׂה. וַיְבָרֶךְ אֱלֹהִים אֶת יוֹם הַשְּׁבִיעִי וַיְקַדֵּשׁ אֹתוֹ, כִּי בוֹ שָׁבַת מִכָּל מְלַאכְתּוֹ, אֲשֶׁר בָּרָא אֱלֹהִים לַעֲשׂוֹת.)

סַבְרִי מָרָנָן וְרַבָּנָן וְרַבּוֹתַי:
בָּרוּךְ אַתָּה יְיָ אֱלֹהֵינוּ מֶלֶךְ הָעוֹלָם, בּוֹרֵא פְּרִי הַגָּפֶן.

בָּרוּךְ אַתָּה יְיָ אֱלֹהֵינוּ מֶלֶךְ הָעוֹלָם, אֲשֶׁר בָּחַר בָּנוּ מִכָּל עַם, ורוממנו מכל לשון, וקדשנו בְּמִצְוֹתָיו. ותתן לנו, יְיָ אֱלֹהֵינוּ אֶת יום (השבת הזה ואת יום) הזכרון הזה, יום זכרון תרועה (בְּאַהֲבָה) מקרא קדש, זֵכֶר לִיצִיאַת מצרים, כִּי בָנוּ בָחַרְתָּ וְאוֹתָנוּ קִדַּשְׁתָּ מִכָּל הָעַמִּים, וּדְבַר אמת וקים לעד.   בָּרוּךְ אַתָּה יְיָ, מְקַדֵּשׁ (הַשַּׁבָּת וּ) ישראל ויום הזכרון.

בָּרוּךְ אַתָּה יְיָ אֱלֹהֵינוּ מֶלֶךְ הָעוֹלָם, שֶׁהֶחֱיָנוּ וְקִיְּמָנוּ וְהִגִּיעָנוּ לַזְּמַן הַזֶּה.

English:

(On Friday night add... *It was evening, then morning of the sixth day and the Heaven and earth were completed, and all their hosts. And on the seventh day God completed the work He had been doing. And God blessed the seventh day and made it holy because on it God ceased His work of creating*).

On Weeknights, begin here, on Shabbat, add the words in parentheses:
Blessed are You, Ado-noy, our God, King of the Universe, Creator of the fruit of the vine.

Blessed are You, Ado-noy, our God, King of the Universe, Who has chosen us from among all nations, elevated us above all tongues, and sanctified us holy through His commandments. And You, Lord our God, have given us in love (this Shabbat day and) this Day of Remembrance, the festival of holy assembly, a day for (the remembrance of) sounding the shofar, (in love,) a holy assembly, commemorating the Exodus from Egypt. For You have chosen us and sanctified us from among all the nations, and Your word, our King, is true and enduring forever. Blessed are You, Ado-noy, King over all the earth, Who sanctifies (the Shabbat and) Israel and the Day of Remembrance.

(When Rosh Hashanah occurs on Saturday night, add the following:
Blessed are You, Ado-noy, our God, King of the Universe, Creator of the lights of fire.

Blessed are You, Ado-noy, our God, King of the Universe , Who distinguishes between holy and the mundane, between light and darkness, between Israel and other nations, between the seventh day and the six working days, between the holiness of Shabbat and the holiness of the festival. Blessed are You, Ado-noy, Who distinguishes between the holy and the holy).

Conclude on all Nights:
Blessed are You, Ado-noy, our God, King of the Universe, Who has granted us life, sustained us and brought us to this occasion.

Transliterated:

(If Rosh Hashanah is on Friday Night, add the following:
Va-y'hee eh-rev, va-y'hee voe-ker yoem ha-shee-she, va-ye-choo-loo ha-sha-ma-yeem v'ha-ah-retz, v'choel tz'va-am. Va-y'chal Elo-heem ba-yoem ha-shvee-ee m'lach-toe ah-sher ah-sah, va-yeesh-boat ba-yoem ha-shvee-ee, mee-coal m'lach-toe ah-sher ah-sah. Va-y'vah-rech Elo-heem eht yoem ha-shvee-ee vah-yee-kah-daish oh-toe, key voeh sha-vat mee-coal m'lach-toe ah-sher bah-rah Elo-heem

la-ah-sow't).

Sav-ree mah-ra-nan v'rah-bah-nan v'rob-oh-tie:

Ba-rooch ah-tah Ado-noy, Elo-hey-noo meh-lech ha-owe-lom, boe-ray pree ha-ga-fen. Ba-rooch ah-ta Ado-noy, Elo-hey-noo me-lech ha-owe-lom, ah-sher ba-char ba-noo mee-coal ahm v'row'm'ma-noo me-coal la-shone, v'keed-sha-noo b'meetz-voe-tav. Va-tee-ten la-noo Ado-noy Elo-hay-noo b'ah-ha-vah. (On Friday Night add… eht yoem ha-shabbat ha-zeh v') eht yoem ha-zee-ka-rown ha-zeh, yoem (On Friday Night add… zeech-rown) true-ah (On Friday Night add…b'ah-ha-vah) meek-rah koe-desh, zay-cher lee-tzee-at meetz-ra-yeem. Key va-noo v'char-tah v'oe-ta-noo key-dash-tah mee-coal hah-ah-meem, ooh-dvar-cha eh-met v'ka-yam la-ahd. Ba-rooch ah-tah Ado-noy, meh-lech ahl coal ha-ah-retz m'ka-daish (On Friday Night add…ha-Shabbat v') Yis-ra-ael v'yoem ha-zee-ka-r'own. Ba-rooch ath-ta Ado-noy, Elo-hey-noo meh-lech ha-owe-lom, sheh-heh-chee-ya-noo v'kee-manoo v'hee-gee-ya-noo lah-z'mon hah-zeh.

Kiddush on Passover, Sukkot & Shavuot

קידוש לשלש רגלים
(לליל שבת)
וַיְהִי עֶרֶב וַיְהִי בֹקֶר
יוֹם הַשִּׁשִּׁי. וַיְכֻלּוּ הַשָּׁמַיִם וְהָאָרֶץ וְכָל צְבָאָם. וַיְכַל אֱלֹהִים בַּיּוֹם הַשְּׁבִיעִי מְלַאכְתּוֹ אֲשֶׁר עָשָׂה, וַיִּשְׁבֹּת בַּיּוֹם הַשְּׁבִיעִי מִכָּל מְלַאכְתּוֹ אֲשֶׁר עָשָׂה. וַיְבָרֶךְ אֱלֹהִים אֶת יוֹם הַשְּׁבִיעִי וַיְקַדֵּשׁ אֹתוֹ, כִּי בוֹ שָׁבַת מִכָּל מְלַאכְתּוֹ, אֲשֶׁר בָּרָא אֱלֹהִים לַעֲשׂוֹת.

סַבְרִי מָרָנָן וְרַבָּנָן וְרַבּוֹתַי
בָּרוּךְ אַתָּה יְיָ אֱלֹהֵינוּ מֶלֶךְ הָעוֹלָם, בּוֹרֵא פְּרִי הַגָּפֶן.

בָּרוּךְ אַתָּה יְיָ אֱלֹהֵינוּ מֶלֶךְ הָעוֹלָם, אֲשֶׁר בָּחַר בָּנוּ מִכָּל עָם וְרוֹמְמָנוּ מִכָּל לָשׁוֹן, וְקִדְּשָׁנוּ בְּמִצְוֹתָיו. וַתִּתֶּן לָנוּ יְיָ אֱלֹהֵינוּ בְּאַהֲבָה (בשבת: שַׁבָּתוֹת לִמְנוּחָה וּ)מוֹעֲדִים לְשִׂמְחָה, חַגִּים וּזְמַנִּים לְשָׂשׂוֹן, אֶת יוֹם (בשבת: הַשַּׁבָּת הַזֶּה וְאֶת יוֹם)
לפסח: חַג הַמַּצּוֹת הַזֶּה, זְמַן חֵרוּתֵנוּ
לשבועות: חַג הַשָּׁבֻעוֹת הַזֶּה, זְמַן מַתַּן תּוֹרָתֵנוּ
לסוכות: חַג הַסֻּכּוֹת הַזֶּה, זְמַן שִׂמְחָתֵנוּ
לשמע"צ ולש"ת: הַשְּׁמִינִי חַג הָעֲצֶרֶת הַזֶּה, זְמַן שִׂמְחָתֵנוּ

Simply Jewish

מִקְרָא קֹדֶשׁ, זֵכֶר לִיצִיאַת מִצְרָיִם. כִּי בָנוּ בָחַרְתָּ
מִכָּל הָעַמִּים, (בשבת: וְשַׁבָּת) וּמוֹעֲדֵי קָדְשֶׁךָ (בשבת: בְּאַהֲבָה)
וְאוֹתָנוּ קִדַּשְׁתָּ
בְּאַהֲבָה וּבְרָצוֹן) בְּשִׂמְחָה וּבְשָׂשׂוֹן הִנְחַלְתָּנוּ. בָּרוּךְ אַתָּה יְיָ, מְקַדֵּשׁ
(בשבת: הַשַּׁבָּת וְ)יִשְׂרָאֵל וְהַזְּמַנִּים.

(בסוכות: בָּרוּךְ אַתָּה יְיָ אֱלֹהֵינוּ מֶלֶךְ הָעוֹלָם, אֲשֶׁר קִדְּשָׁנוּ בְּמִצְוֹתָיו,
וְצִוָּנוּ לֵישֵׁב בַּסֻּכָּה.)

English:

(On Friday night) *it was evening, then morning of the sixth day and the Heaven and earth were completed, and all their hosts. And on the seventh day God completed the work He had been doing. And God blessed the seventh day and made it holy because on it God ceased His work of creating).*

On Weeknights, begin here (and on Friday Night add the words in parentheses):

Blessed are You, Ado-noy, our God, King of the Universe, Creator of the fruit of the vine.

Blessed are You, Ado-noy, our God, King of the Universe, Who chose us from all the nations, and elevated us above all tongues, and sanctified us with His commandments. And You, Lord our God, have given us with love, [Sabbaths for rest and] festivals for happiness, holidays and times for joy, this day [of Shabbat and this day of]

(on Passover) *the Festival of Matzos, the time of our freedom,*

(on Shavuot) *the Festival of Weeks, the time of the giving of our Torah,*

(on Sukkot) *the festival of Sukkot, the time of our happiness,*

(on Shemini Atzeret/Simchat Torah) *the eighth day, the Festival of Assembly, the time of our happiness,*

[With love], a holy assmbly, a remembrance of the Exodus from Egypt. Because You chose us, and sanctified us from all the nations, [and Shabbat] and Your holy festivals [in love and in favor] in happiness and in joy, You have given us as a heritage. Blessed are You, Ado-noy, Who sanctifies [the Shabbat,] and Israel and the holiday seasons.

(On Sukkot, if eating in the Sukkah, the following blessing is added after kiddush:

Blessed are You, Ado-noy, our God, King of the Universe, Who has sanctified us with His commandments and commanded us to dwell in the Sukkah).

Conclude on all Nights:

Blessed are You, Ado-noy, our God, King of the Universe, Who has granted us life, sustained us and brought us to this occasion.

Transliterated:

(On Friday night) Va-y'hee eh-rev, va-y'hee voe-ker yoem ha-she-she, va-y'choo-loo ha-sha-ma-yeem v'ha-ah-retz, v'choal tz'va-am. Va-y'chal Elo-heem ba-yoem ha-shvee-ee m'lach-toe ah-sher ah-sah, va-yeesh-boat ba-yoem ha-shvee-ee, mee-coal m'lach-toe ah-sher ah-sah. Va-y'vah-rech Elo-heem eht yoem ha-shvee-ee vah-yee-kah-daish oh-toe, key voeh sha-vat mee-coal m'lach-toe ah-sher bah-rah Elo-heem la-ah-sow't).

Sav-ree mah-ra-non v'rah-bah-nan v'rob-oh-tie:
Ba-rooch ah-tah Ado-noy, Elo-hey-noo meh-lech ha-owe-lom, boe-ray pree ha-ga-fen. Ba-rooch ah-ta Ado-noy, Elo-hey-noo meh-lech ha-owe-lom, ah-sher ba-char ba-noo mee-coal ahm v'row'm'ma-noo me-coal la-shone, v'keed-sha-noo b'meetz-voe-tav.
Va-tee-ten la-noo Ado-noy Elo-hay-noo b'ah-ha-vah. **(On Friday Night add**…eht yoem ha-Shabbat ha-zeh v'eht yoem:)
(on Passover) chog ha-Matzot ha-zeh, zmon chay-roo-tay-noo,
(on Shavuot) chog ha-Shavoo-oat ha-zeh, zman ma-ton toe-ra-tay-noo.
(on Sukkot) chog ha-Sue-coat ha-zeh, zmon sim-cha-tay-noo,
(on Shemini Atzeret/Simchat Torah): ha-Shmee-nee chog ha-atzeret ha-zeh, zman simcha-tay-noo,
(On Friday Night add…b'ah-ha-vah) meek-rah koe-desh, zay-cher lee-tzee-ot meetz-ra-yeem. Key va-noo v'char-tah v'oh-ta-noo key-dash-tah mee-coal hah-ah-meem,
(on Friday night add…v'Shabbat) ooh-moe-ah-day kad-sheh-cha
(on Friday night add…b'ah-ha-va ooh-v'ra-tzown), b'seem-cha ooh-v'sa-sown heen-chal-ta-noo. Ba-rooch ah-tah Ado-noy, m'ka-daish
(On Friday Night add…ha-Shabbat v') Yis-ra-ael v'ha-zma-neem.
(On Sukkot, if eating in the Sukka, the following blessing is added after kiddush:
Ba-rooch ah-ta Ado-noy, Elo-hey-noo meh-lech ha-owe-lom, ah-sher kid-sha-noo b'meetz-voe-tav, v'tzee'va-noo lay-shave ba-sue-ka).

Conclude on all Nights:

Ba-rooch ath-ta Ado-noy, Elo-hey-noo meh-lech ha-owe-lom, sheh-heh-chee-ya-noo v'kee-ma-noo v'hee-gee-ya-noo lah-zmon hah-zeh.

Blessings on the Lulav

Hebrew: בָּרוּךְ אַתָּה יְיָ אֱלֹהֵינוּ מֶלֶךְ הָעוֹלָם, אֲשֶׁר קִדְּשָׁנוּ בְּמִצְוֹתָיו, וְצִוָּנוּ עַל נְטִילַת לוּלָב.

בפעם הראשונה מוסיף:
בָּרוּךְ אַתָּה יְיָ אֱלֹהֵינוּ מֶלֶךְ הָעוֹלָם, שֶׁהֶחֱיָנוּ וְקִיְּמָנוּ וְהִגִּיעָנוּ לַזְּמַן הַזֶּה.

(בסוכות: בָּרוּךְ אַתָּה יְיָ אֱלֹהֵינוּ מֶלֶךְ הָעוֹלָם, אֲשֶׁר קִדְּשָׁנוּ בְּמִצְוֹתָיו וְצִוָּנוּ לֵישֵׁב בַּסֻּכָּה.)

English: *Blessed are You, Ado-noy, our God, King of the Universe, Who has sanctified us with His commandments, and commanded us regarding the waving of the Lulav.*

(On the first lulav blessing of the season add):
Blessed are You, Ado-noy, our God, King of the Universe, Who has granted us life, sustained us and brought us to this occasion.

(Whenever you eat in the Sukkah add the following blessing):
Blessed are You, Ado-noy, our God, King of the Universe, Who has sanctified us with His commandments and commanded us to dwell in the Sukkah.

Transliterated: Ba-rooch ah-ta Ado-noy, Elo-hey-noo meh-lech ha-owe-lom, ah-sher kid-sha-noo b'meetz-voe-tav v'zee-va-noo ahl n'tee-lot loo-lahv.

(On the first lulav blessing of the season add): Ba-rooh ah-ta Ado-noy, Elo-hey-noo meh-lech ha-owe-lom, sheh-heh-chee-ya-noo v'key-ma-noo v'hee-gee-ya-noo lah-zmon hah-zeh.

(Whenever you eat in the Sukkah add the following blessing): Ba-rooch ah-ta Ado-noy, Elo-hey-noo meh-lech ha-owe-lom, ah-sher kid-sha-noo b'meetz-voe-tov v'zee-va-noo lay-shave ba-sue-ka.

RESOURCE VI
Chanukah

Blessings When Lighting the Menorah

Hebrew:

בָּרוּךְ אַתָּה יְיָ אֱלֹהֵינוּ מֶלֶךְ הָעוֹלָם, אֲשֶׁר קִדְּשָׁנוּ בְּמִצְוֹתָיו, וְצִוָּנוּ
לְהַדְלִיק נֵר שֶׁל חֲנֻכָּה.

בָּרוּךְ אַתָּה יְיָ אֱלֹהֵינוּ מֶלֶךְ הָעוֹלָם, שֶׁעָשָׂה נִסִּים לַאֲבוֹתֵינוּ בַּיָּמִים
הָהֵם בַּזְּמַן הַזֶּה.

בערב הראשון מוסיפים גם "שהחיינו":

בָּרוּךְ אַתָּה יְיָ אֱלֹהֵינוּ מֶלֶךְ הָעוֹלָם, שֶׁהֶחֱיָנוּ וְקִיְּמָנוּ וְהִגִּיעָנוּ לַזְּמַן הַזֶּה.

אחר ההדלקה יאמר:

הַנֵּרוֹת הַלָּלוּ אֲנַחְנוּ מַדְלִיקִים עַל הַנִּסִּים וְעַל הַנִּפְלָאוֹת וְעַל הַתְּשׁוּעוֹת
וְעַל הַמִּלְחָמוֹת, שֶׁעָשִׂיתָ לַאֲבוֹתֵינוּ בַּיָּמִים הָהֵם בַּזְּמַן הַזֶּה, עַל יְדֵי
כֹּהֲנֶיךָ הַקְּדוֹשִׁים. וְכָל שְׁמוֹנַת יְמֵי חֲנֻכָּה הַנֵּרוֹת הַלָּלוּ קֹדֶשׁ הֵם, וְאֵין
לָנוּ רְשׁוּת לְהִשְׁתַּמֵּשׁ בָּהֶם, אֶלָּא לִרְאוֹתָם בִּלְבָד, כְּדֵי לְהוֹדוֹת וּלְהַלֵּל
לְשִׁמְךָ הַגָּדוֹל, עַל נִסֶּיךָ וְעַל נִפְלְאוֹתֶיךָ וְעַל יְשׁוּעָתֶךָ.

English:

*Blessed are You, Ado-noy, our God, King of the Universe, Who has
sanctified us with His commandments, and commanded us to light
Chanukah candles.*

*Blessed are You, Ado-noy, our God, King of the Universe, Who has
performed miracles for our fathers in this season, in those days.*

(On the first night add): *Blessed are You, Ado-noy, our God, King of
the Universe, Who has granted us life, sustained us and brought us to
this occasion.*

Transliterated:
Ba-rooch ah-ta Ado-noy, Elo-hey-noo meh-lech
ha-owe-lom, ah-sher kid-sha-noo b'meetz-voe-tav v'zee-va-noo
l'hod-leak nair shel Cha-new-ka.

Ba-rooch ah-ta Ado-noy, Elo-hey-noo meh-lech ha-owe-lom, sheh-ah-sah nee-seem la-ah-voe-tay-noo ba-ya-meem ha-haim ba-zmon hah-zeh.

(Only recited on the first night): Ba-rooch ah-ta Ado-noy, Elo-hey-noo meh-lech ha-owe-lom, sheh-heh-chee-ya-noo v'kee-ma-noo v'hee-gee-ya-noo lah-zmon hah-zeh.

Rock of Ages

Hebrew:

מָעוֹז צוּר יְשׁוּעָתִי
לְךָ נָאֶה לְשַׁבֵּחַ,
תְּכוֹן בֵּית תְּפִלָּתִי
וְשָׁם תּוֹדָה נְזַבֵּחַ,
לְעֵת תָּכִין מַטְבֵּחַ
מִצָּר הַמְנַבֵּחַ,
אָז אֶגְמֹר
בְּשִׁיר מִזְמוֹר
חֲנֻכַּת הַמִּזְבֵּחַ.

רָעוֹת שָׂבְעָה נַפְשִׁי
בְּיָגוֹן כֹּחִי כָּלָה,
חַיַּי מֵרְרוּ בְקֹשִׁי
בְּשִׁעְבּוּד מַלְכוּת עֶגְלָה,
וּבְיָדוֹ הַגְּדוֹלָה
הוֹצִיא אֶת הַסְּגֻלָּה,
חֵיל פַּרְעֹה
וְכָל זַרְעוֹ
יָרְדוּ כְאֶבֶן מְצוּלָה.

דְּבִיר קָדְשׁוֹ הֱבִיאַנִי
וְגַם שָׁם לֹא שָׁקַטְתִּי,
וּבָא נוֹגֵשׂ וְהִגְלַנִי,
כִּי זָרִים עָבַדְתִּי,
וְיַיִן רַעַל מָסַכְתִּי
כִּמְעַט שֶׁעָבַרְתִּי,
קֵץ בָּבֶל,
זְרֻבָּבֶל,
לְקֵץ שִׁבְעִים נוֹשַׁעְתִּי.

כְּרֹת קוֹמַת בְּרוֹשׁ בִּקֵּשׁ
אֲגָגִי בֶּן הַמְּדָתָא,
וְנִהְיָתָה לוֹ לְפַח וּלְמוֹקֵשׁ
וְגַאֲוָתוֹ נִשְׁבָּתָה,
רֹאשׁ יְמִינִי נִשֵּׂאתָ,
וְאוֹיֵב שְׁמוֹ מָחִיתָ,
רֹב בָּנָיו
וְקִנְיָנָיו
עַל הָעֵץ תָּלִיתָ.

יְוָנִים נִקְבְּצוּ עָלַי
אֲזַי בִּימֵי חַשְׁמַנִּים,
וּפָרְצוּ חוֹמוֹת מִגְדָּלַי
וְטִמְּאוּ כָּל הַשְּׁמָנִים,
וּמִנּוֹתַר קַנְקַנִּים
נַעֲשָׂה נֵס לַשּׁוֹשַׁנִּים,
בְּנֵי בִינָה
יְמֵי שְׁמוֹנָה
קָבְעוּ שִׁיר וּרְנָנִים.

חֲשׂוֹף זְרוֹעַ קָדְשֶׁךָ
וְקָרֵב קֵץ הַיְשׁוּעָה,
נְקֹם נִקְמַת דַּם עֲבָדֶיךָ
מֵאֻמָּה הָרְשָׁעָה,

כִּי אָרְכָה לָּנוּ הַיְשׁוּעָה,
דְּחֵה אַדְמוֹן

וְאֵין קֵץ לִימֵי הָרָעָה,
בְּצֵל צַלְמוֹן
הָקֵם לָנוּ רוֹעִים שִׁבְעָה.

English: *Rock of Ages, my salvation, it is so fitting to praise You. Restore the House of my prayers and there we will bring thanksgiving offerings. When You slaughter the blaspheming enemy, I will complete the dedication of the altar, with a song of praise.*

My soul was full of troubles, sorrow sapped my strength. My life was made bitter from the harsh bondage of the calf-like kingdom. But with His mighty hand He took out the treasured ones. Pharoh's army and all his offspring sank like a rock into the deep.

He brought me to His holy place, but there too I could not rest. A tormentor came and exiled me for I served strange (gods) and drank intoxicating wine. Shortly after I left, Babylonia ceased, Zerubavel came, and at the end of the seventy (years) I was saved.

The Aggagi, son of Hamdatta, tried to uproot the towering cypress, but it became a trap and stumbling block to him and his arrogance ceased. You lifted the head of the Benjaminite, and the enemy, may his name be erased, You hung on the gallows, together with his (possessions) many sons.

In the days of the Chashmona'eem, the Greeks gathered against me. They breeched the walls of my towers, and defiled all the oils. And from the sole remaining container You performed a miracle for the roses. Men of understanding set eight days for song and joy.

Uncover Your holy arm and bring the end, the salvation. Avenge the blood of your servants from the evil nation. For we have waited so long for the salvation, and there is no end to the days of evil. Push the red one from inner shadow and establish the seven shepherds.

Transliterated:
Ma-owes tzur y'shoo-ah-tee, L'cha na-eh l'sha-bay-ach.
Tee-cone bait t'fee-la-tee v'shom toe-da n'za-bay-ach.

L'ate ta-cheen mot-bay-ach me-tzar ha-m'na-bay-ach,
oz egg-more b'sheer meez-more cha-new-cot ha-meez-bay-ach.

Ra-oat sav-ah naf-she b'ya-g'own koe-chee ka-lah,
cha-yai may-roo v'co-she b'she-bewd mahl-choot egg-la,
ooh-v'ya-doe ha-g'doe-la hoe-tzee eht ha-s'goo-la,
chail Par-oh v'choal zar-oh yar-dew k'eh-ven m'tzue-la.

Dveer cod-show hevee-ah-nee v'gom shom low sha-kat'tee,
ooh-vah no-gais v'heeg-la-nee key za-reem ah-vad'd-tee,
v'yain ra-ahl ma-sach-tee keem-aht sheh-ah-var-tee,
kay'tz Ba-vehl, Z'roo-ba-vehl, l'kay'tz sheeve-eem no-shah-tee.

K'row't coe-maht b'row'sh bee-kay'sh Ah-ga-gee ben Ham-da-tah,
v'nee-ta low l'fah'ch ooh-l'moe-kay'sh v'ga-ah-va-toe neesh-ba-ta,
row'sh Y'mee-nee nee-say-ta v'oh-yaiv shmoe ma-chee-ta,
row'v ba-nov v'keen-ya-nov ahl ha-aytz ta-lee-ta.

Y'va-neem neek-b'sue ah-lie ah-z'eye bee-may Chash-ma-neem,
ooh-far-sue choe-moat meeg-da-lie v'teem-ooh coal ha-shma-neem,
ooh-me-no-tar con-ka-neem nah-ah-sah nais la-show-sha-neem,
b'nay vee-nah y'may shmoe-nah kav-ooh sheer ooh'r'na-neem.

Cha-sowf z'row-ah cod-sheh-cha, v'ka-rave kay'tz ha-y'shoo-ah,
n'koem neek-maht ah-va-de-cha may-ooh-mah ha-r-sha-ah,
key ar-chah la-noo ha-y'shoo-ah v'ain kay'tz l'may ha-ra-ah,
d'chay ad-moan b'tsail tzal-moan ha-keem la-noo roe-eem sheeve-
ah.

RESOURCE VII
Ceremonies Involving Babies

Naming a Daughter

Hebrew:

מי שברך ליולדת וקריאת השם

מִי שֶׁבֵּרַךְ אֲבוֹתֵינוּ אַבְרָהָם יִצְחָק וְיַעֲקֹב, הוֹא יְבָרֵךְ אֶת הָאִשָּׁה הַיּוֹלֶדֶת
(פלונית בַּת)פלוני וְאֶת בִּתָּה הַנּוֹלְדָה לָהּ בְּמַזָּל טוֹב,
וְיִקָּרֵא שְׁמָהּ בְּיִשְׂרָאֵל פלונית בַּת פלוני,
בַּעֲבוּר שֶׁבַּעְלָהּ וְאָבִיהָ יִתֵּן לִצְדָקָה. בִּשְׂכַר זֶה, יִגְדְּלָה לְתוֹרָה
וּלְחֻפָּה וּלְמַעֲשִׂים טוֹבִים. וְנֹאמַר אָמֵן.

English:
*May the One Who blessed our forefathers, Abraham, Isaac, and Jacob,
bless the woman who has given birth _____ (mother's
Hebrew name), the daughter of _____(father's Hebrew
name), together with her daughter who has been born at an auspicious
time. May her name be called in Israel _____ (baby's
Hebrew Name), daughter of _____ (baby's father's Hebrew
name). On her behalf, her husband, the infant's father will contribute
to charity. In reward for this, may they raise her to Torah, marriage,
and good deeds. Now let us say: AMEN.*

Transliterated: Me sheh-bay-rah'ch ah-voe-tay-noo, Av-ra-hom,
Yitz-chok, v'Ya-cove, who y'va-ray'ch eht ha-ee-shah ho-yoe-
leh-det _____ bot _____ v'eht bee-tah ha-nole-da lah
b'ma-zal toe've, v'yee-ka-ray sh'mah b'yis-ra-ael _____ bot
_____, ba-ah-voor sheh-ba-lah, v'ah-vee-hah yee-tain l'tz'da-
kah, bee-s'chor zeh, y'god-lah l'Toe-rah ooh-l'choo-pah ooh-l'ma-
seem toe-veem, v'no-mar, ah-main.

The Bris / Circumcision

Hebrew:

כשמכניסים את התינוק למול אומר הקהל: בָּרוּךְ הַבָּא.
וַיְדַבֵּר יְיָ אֶל מֹשֶׁה לֵּאמֹר. פִּינְחָס בֶּן אֶלְעָזָר בֶּן אַהֲרֹן הַכֹּהֵן הֵשִׁיב אֶת
חֲמָתִי מֵעַל בְּנֵי יִשְׂרָאֵל, בְּקַנְאוֹ אֶת קִנְאָתִי בְּתוֹכָם, וְלֹא כִלִּיתִי אֶת בְּנֵי
יִשְׂרָאֵל בְּקִנְאָתִי. לָכֵן אֱמֹר, הִנְנִי נֹתֵן לוֹ אֶת בְּרִיתִי שָׁלוֹם.
שָׂמִים את התינוק על הכסא של אליהו, והמוהל אומר:
זֶה הַכִּסֵּא שֶׁל אֵלִיָּהוּ הַנָּבִיא זָכוּר לַטּוֹב.
לִישׁוּעָתְךָ קִוִּיתִי יְיָ. שִׂבַּרְתִּי לִישׁוּעָתְךָ יְיָ, וּמִצְוֹתֶיךָ עָשִׂיתִי. אֵלִיָּהוּ מַלְאַךְ
הַבְּרִית, הִנֵּה שֶׁלְּךָ לְפָנֶיךָ, עֲמֹד עַל יְמִינִי וְסָמְכֵנִי. שִׂבַּרְתִּי לִישׁוּעָתְךָ יְיָ.
שָׂשׂ אָנֹכִי עַל אִמְרָתֶךָ, כְּמוֹצֵא שָׁלָל רָב. שָׁלוֹם רָב לְאֹהֲבֵי תוֹרָתֶךָ, וְאֵין
לָמוֹ מִכְשׁוֹל. אַשְׁרֵי תִּבְחַר וּתְקָרֵב יִשְׁכֹּן חֲצֵרֶיךָ,
כל הקהל אומרים: נִשְׂבְּעָה בְּטוּב בֵּיתֶךָ קְדֹשׁ הֵיכָלֶךָ.

אומר אבי הבן: הִנְנִי מוּכָן וּמְזֻמָּן לְקַיֵּם מִצְוַת עֲשֵׂה שֶׁצִּוָּנִי הַבּוֹרֵא
יִתְבָּרַךְ, לָמוּל אֶת בְּנִי.

המוהל אומר: אָמַר הַקָּדוֹשׁ בָּרוּךְ הוּא לְאַבְרָהָם אָבִינוּ, הִתְהַלֵּךְ לְפָנַי
וֶהְיֵה תָמִים. הִנְנִי מוּכָן וּמְזֻמָּן לְקַיֵּם מִצְוַת עֲשֵׂה שֶׁצִּוָּנוּ הַבּוֹרֵא יִתְבָּרַךְ,
לָמוּל.

שמים את התינוק על ברכי הסנדק והמוהל מברך:
ברכות המילה
בָּרוּךְ אַתָּה יְיָ אֱלֹהֵינוּ מֶלֶךְ הָעוֹלָם, אֲשֶׁר קִדְּשָׁנוּ בְּמִצְוֹתָיו, וְצִוָּנוּ עַל
הַמִּילָה.

ומיד אחרי המילה אבי הבן מברך:
בָּרוּךְ אַתָּה יְיָ אֱלֹהֵינוּ מֶלֶךְ הָעוֹלָם, אֲשֶׁר קִדְּשָׁנוּ בְּמִצְוֹתָיו, וְצִוָּנוּ
לְהַכְנִיסוֹ בִּבְרִיתוֹ שֶׁל אַבְרָהָם אָבִינוּ.

וכל העומדים שם עונים:
אָמֵן. כְּשֵׁם שֶׁנִּכְנַס לַבְּרִית, כֵּן יִכָּנֵס לְתוֹרָה וּלְחֻפָּה וּלְמַעֲשִׂים טוֹבִים.

ואחר גמר המילה מברכים על כוס יין:
בָּרוּךְ אַתָּה יְיָ אֱלֹהֵינוּ מֶלֶךְ הָעוֹלָם, בּוֹרֵא פְּרִי הַגָּפֶן.
בָּרוּךְ אַתָּה יְיָ אֱלֹהֵינוּ מֶלֶךְ הָעוֹלָם, אֲשֶׁר קִדַּשׁ יְדִיד מִבֶּטֶן, וְחֹק בִּשְׁאֵרוֹ
שָׂם, וְצֶאֱצָאָיו חָתַם בְּאוֹת בְּרִית קֹדֶשׁ. עַל כֵּן בִּשְׂכַר זֹאת, אֵל חַי,
חֶלְקֵנוּ, צוּרֵנוּ, צַוֵּה לְהַצִּיל יְדִידוּת שְׁאֵרֵנוּ מִשַּׁחַת, לְמַעַן בְּרִיתוֹ אֲשֶׁר
שָׂם בִּבְשָׂרֵנוּ. בָּרוּךְ אַתָּה יְיָ, כּוֹרֵת הַבְּרִית.

אֱלֹהֵינוּ וֵאלֹהֵי אֲבוֹתֵינוּ, קַיֵּם אֶת הַיֶּלֶד הַזֶּה לְאָבִיו וּלְאִמּוֹ, וְיִקָּרֵא שְׁמוֹ בְּיִשְׂרָאֵל (_____ בֶּן _____). יִשְׂמַח הָאָב בְּיוֹצֵא חֲלָצָיו וְתָגֵל אִמּוֹ בִּפְרִי בִטְנָהּ, כַּכָּתוּב: יִשְׂמַח אָבִיךָ וְאִמֶּךָ, וְתָגֵל יוֹלַדְתֶּךָ. וְנֶאֱמַר: וָאֶעֱבֹר עָלַיִךְ וָאֶרְאֵךְ מִתְבּוֹסֶסֶת בְּדָמָיִךְ, וָאֹמַר לָךְ בְּדָמַיִךְ חֲיִי, וָאֹמַר לָךְ בְּדָמַיִךְ חֲיִי. וְנֶאֱמַר: זָכַר לְעוֹלָם בְּרִיתוֹ, דָּבָר צִוָּה לְאֶלֶף דּוֹר. אֲשֶׁר כָּרַת אֶת אַבְרָהָם, וּשְׁבוּעָתוֹ לְיִצְחָק. וַיַּעֲמִידֶהָ לְיַעֲקֹב לְחֹק, לְיִשְׂרָאֵל בְּרִית עוֹלָם. וְנֶאֱמַר: וַיָּמָל אַבְרָהָם אֶת יִצְחָק בְּנוֹ בֶּן שְׁמֹנַת יָמִים, כַּאֲשֶׁר צִוָּה אֹתוֹ אֱלֹהִים. הוֹדוּ לַיְיָ כִּי טוֹב, כִּי לְעוֹלָם חַסְדּוֹ. הוֹדוּ לַיְיָ כִּי טוֹב, כִּי לְעוֹלָם חַסְדּוֹ. (_____ בֶּן _____) זֶה הַקָּטֹן גָּדוֹל יִהְיֶה, כְּשֵׁם שֶׁנִּכְנַס לַבְּרִית, כֵּן יִכָּנֵס לְתוֹרָה וּלְחֻפָּה וּלְמַעֲשִׂים טוֹבִים.

זִמּוּן לִסְעוּדַת בְּרִית מִילָה

הַמְזַמֵּן אוֹמֵר: רַבּוֹתַי, נְבָרֵךְ.

הַמְסֻבִּים עוֹנִים: יְהִי שֵׁם יְיָ מְבֹרָךְ מֵעַתָּה וְעַד עוֹלָם.

וְהַמְזַמֵּן חוֹזֵר: יְהִי שֵׁם יְיָ מְבֹרָךְ מֵעַתָּה וְעַד עוֹלָם.

נוֹדֶה לְשִׁמְךָ בְּתוֹךְ אֱמוּנַי, בְּרוּכִים אַתֶּם לַיְיָ.

בִּרְשׁוּת אֵל אָיֹם וְנוֹרָא,   מִשְׂגָּב לְעִתּוֹת בַּצָּרָה,

אֵל נֶאְזָר בִּגְבוּרָה,   אַדִּיר בַּמָּרוֹם יְיָ.

נוֹדֶה לְשִׁמְךָ בְּתוֹךְ אֱמוּנַי, בְּרוּכִים אַתֶּם לַיְיָ.

בִּרְשׁוּת הַתּוֹרָה הַקְּדוֹשָׁה,   טְהוֹרָה הִיא וְגַם פְּרוּשָׁה,

צִוָּה לָנוּ מוֹרָשָׁה,   מֹשֶׁה עֶבֶד יְיָ.

נוֹדֶה לְשִׁמְךָ בְּתוֹךְ אֱמוּנַי, בְּרוּכִים אַתֶּם לַיְיָ.

בִּרְשׁוּת הַכֹּהֲנִים וְהַלְוִיִּם,   אֶקְרָא לֵאלֹהֵי הָעִבְרִים,

אֲהוֹדֶנּוּ בְּכָל אִיִּים,   אֲבָרְכָה אֶת יְיָ.

נוֹדֶה לְשִׁמְךָ בְּתוֹךְ אֱמוּנַי, בְּרוּכִים אַתֶּם לַיְיָ.

בִּרְשׁוּת מָרָנָן וְרַבּוֹתַי,   אֶפְתְּחָה בְּשִׁיר פִּי וּשְׂפָתַי,

וְתֹאמַרְנָה עַצְמוֹתַי,   בָּרוּךְ הַבָּא בְּשֵׁם יְיָ.

נוֹדֶה לְשִׁמְךָ בְּתוֹךְ אֱמוּנַי, בְּרוּכִים אַתֶּם לַיְיָ. בִּרְשׁוּת מָרָנָן וְכוּ׳

כְּשֶׁמַּגִּיעַ הַמְזַמֵּן אֶל "בְּעֵינֵי אֱלֹהִים וְאָדָם" יֹאמַר:

הָרַחֲמָן הוּא יְבָרֵךְ אֲבִי הַיֶּלֶד וְאִמּוֹ, וְיִזְכּוּ לְגַדְּלוֹ וּלְחַנְּכוֹ וּלְחַכְּמוֹ, מִיּוֹם הַשְּׁמִינִי וָהָלְאָה יֵרָצֶה דָמוֹ, וִיהִי יְיָ אֱלֹהָיו עִמּוֹ.

הָרַחֲמָן הוּא יְבָרֵךְ בַּעַל בְּרִית הַמִּילָה, אֲשֶׁר שָׂשׂ לַעֲשׂוֹת צֶדֶק בְּגִילָה, וִישַׁלֵּם פָּעֳלוֹ וּמַשְׂכֻּרְתּוֹ כְּפוּלָה, וְיִתְּנֵהוּ לְמַעְלָה לְמָעְלָה.

הָרַחֲמָן הוּא יְבָרֵךְ רַךְ הַנִּמּוֹל לִשְׁמוֹנָה, וְיִהְיוּ יָדָיו וְלִבּוֹ לָאֵל אֱמוּנָה, וְיִזְכֶּה לִרְאוֹת פְּנֵי הַשְּׁכִינָה, שָׁלֹשׁ פְּעָמִים בַּשָּׁנָה.

הָרַחֲמָן הוּא יְבָרֵךְ הַמָּל בְּשַׂר הָעָרְלָה, וּפָרַע וּמָצַץ דְּמֵי הַמִּילָה, אִישׁ הַיָּרֵא וְרַךְ הַלֵּבָב עֲבוֹדָתוֹ פְּסוּלָה, אִם שְׁלָשׁ אֵלֶּה לֹא יַעֲשֶׂה לָהּ.

הָרַחֲמָן הוּא יִשְׁלַח לָנוּ מְשִׁיחוֹ הוֹלֵךְ תָּמִים, בִּזְכוּת חֲתַן לַמּוּלוֹת דָּמִים, לְבַשֵּׂר בְּשׂוֹרוֹת טוֹבוֹת וְנִחוּמִים, לְעַם אֶחָד מְפֻזָּר וּמְפֹרָד בֵּין הָעַמִּים.

הָרַחֲמָן הוּא יִשְׁלַח לָנוּ כֹהֵן צֶדֶק אֲשֶׁר לֻקַּח לְעֵילָם, עַד הוּכַן כִּסְאוֹ כַּשֶּׁמֶשׁ וְיָהֲלֹם, וַיָּלֶט פָּנָיו בְּאַדַּרְתּוֹ וַיִּגְלֹם, בְּרִיתִי הָיְתָה אִתּוֹ הַחַיִּים וְהַשָּׁלוֹם. וּמַמְשִׁיכִים "הָרַחֲמָן" וְכוּ׳

English:

When the baby enters all present say:
Blessed is the one who has entered.

When the baby is placed on the chair of Elijah, the Mohel says:
This is the chair of Elijah the Prophet, may he be remembered for good.
The father says: *I am now prepared to fulfill the positive command of the Creator, may He be blessed, to circumcise my son.*
The Mohel says: *I am now prepared to fulfill the positive command of the Creator, may He be blessed, to perform the circumcision.*

The baby is held on the Sandek and the Mohel recites the following blessing: *Blessed are You, Ado-noy, our God, King of the Universe, Who has sanctified us with His commandments, and commanded us concerning circumcision.*

Immediately after the Mohel performs the bris, the father recites the following blessing:
Blessed are You, Ado-noy, our God, King of the Universe, Who has sanctified us with His commandments, and commanded us to enter him (our son) into the Covenant of Abraham, our father.
All present respond: *Amen. Just as he has entered into the Covenant, so may he enter into Torah, into marriage, and into good deeds.*

The following Blessings are recited:
(Over a glass of wine). *Blessed are You, Ado-noy, our God, King of the Universe, Who creates the fruit of the vine.*
Blessed are You, Ado-noy, our God, King of the Universe, Who sanctified the beloved one from the womb, set His statute in his flesh, and sealed his descendants with the sign of the holy Covenant. Therefore, as a reward for this circumcision, living God, our Portion, and our Rock, may You issue the command that our flesh be saved from the abyss, for the sake of the Covenant which He has set in our flesh. Blessed are You, Ado-noy, Who makes the Covenant.

Amidst the following prayer, the baby's name is given:
Our God, and God of our fathers, preserve this child for his father and for his mother, and may his name in Israel be called _____ (say the baby's Hebrew name), the son of _____(say the father's Hebrew name). May the father rejoice in his offspring, and his mother be gladdened with the fruit of her womb, as it is written: "May your father and mother rejoice, and she who bore you be glad". As it is said: "I passed by and saw you amidst your blood, and I said to you,' through your blood, you shall

live.'; and I said to you, 'through your blood, you shall live.". And it is said: "He has remembered His Covenant forever, the word which He has commanded to a thousand generations; the Covenant which He made with Abraham, and His oath to Isaac; He established it for Jacob as a statute, for Israel as an everlasting Covenant". And it is said: "Abraham circumcised his son Isaac when he was eight days old, as God had commanded him". Give thanks to Ado-noy, for He is good, for His kindness is everlasting. Give thanks to the Lord for He is good, because His kindness is everlasting. May this little one _____(say the baby's Hebrew name) *the son of* _____ (say the father's Hebrew name), *become great. Just as he has entered the Covenant, so may he enter into Torah, into marriage, and into good deeds.*

After naming the child, the person who recited the blessings drinks the wine. The mohel and the father recite the following prayer.
Master of the Universe, may it be Your will that this circumcision be regarded and accepted by You as if I had offered him before the Throne of Your Glory. And You, in Your abounding mercy, send through Your holy angels a holy and pure soul to _____(say the baby's Hebrew name) *the son of* _____ (say the father's Hebrew name), *who has now been circumcised for the sake of Your great Name. May his heart be open to Your holy Torah, to learn and to teach, to observe and to practice. Grant him long life, a life imbued with the fear of sin, a life of wealth and honor; and may he fulfill the desires of his heart for good. Amen, and so may it be Your will.*
The mohel then recites the following:
May He who blessed our fathers, Abraham, Isaac and Jacob, Moses and Aaron, David and Solomon, bless this tender infant _____ (say the baby's Hebrew name) *the son of* _____ *(say the father's Hebrew name).* _____(say the father's Hebrew name) *the son of* _____(say his father's name, the grandfather's Hebrew name), *pledged charity for his sake for bikkur cholim. In this merit, may the Holy One, blessed be He, hasten to send a complete recovery to all his two hundred forty-eight bodily parts and three hundred sixty-five veins, and raise him to Torah, to marriage, and to good deeds; and let us say, Amen.*

The festive meal follows, it is concluded with the Grace After Meals.

Transliterated:
When the baby enters all present say: Ba-rooch ha-bah.

When the baby is placed on the chair of Elijah, the Mohel says: Zeh ha-key-say shell Eli-ya-hoo Ha-na-vee, za-chor la-toe've.

Simply Jewish

The father says: He-n'nee moo-chon ooh-m'zoo-mon l'ka-yay'm meetz-vot ah-say sheh-tzee-va-nee ha-boe-ray yeet-ba-rach, la-mool eht b'nee.

The Mohel says: He-n'nee moo-chon ooh-m'zoo-mon l'ka-yay'm meetz-vot ah-say sheh-tzee-va-nee ha-boe-ray yeet-ba-rach, la-mool. The baby is held on the Sandek and the Mohel recites the following blessing:
Ba-rooch ah-ta Ado-noy, Elo-hey-noo meh-lech ha-owe-lom, ah-sher kid-sha-noo b'meetz-voe-tav, v'zee-va-noo ahl ha-mee-lah.

Immediately after the Mohel performs the bris, the father recites the following blessing:
Ba-rooch ah-ta Ado-noy, Elo-hey-noo meh-lech ha-owe-lom, ah-sher kid-sha-noo b'meetz-voe-tav, v'zee-va-noo l'hoch-nee-so bee'v-ree-toe shell Av-ra-hom ah-vee-noo.

All present respond: Ah-main. K'shame sheh-neech-noss la-breet, cain yee-ca-nais la-breet, cain yee-ca-nais l'Toe-rah, ooh-l'choo-pah, ooh-l'ma-seem toe-veem.
The following Blessings are recited:
(Over a glass of wine).
Ba-rooch ah-tah Ado-noy, Elo-hey-noo meh-lech ha-oe-lahm, boe-ray pree ha-ga-fen.
Ba-rooch ah-tah Ado-noy, Elo-hey-noo meh-lech ha-oe-lahm, ah-sher kee-dosh y'deed me-beh-ten, v'choke beesh-ay-row sohm, v'tzeh-eh-tza-ov cha-tom b'oat breet ko-desh. Ahl cain bees-chor z'oat, Ail chai, chel-kay-noo, tzoo-ray-noo, tza-vay l'ha-t'seal y'dee-doot sh-ay-ray-noo mee-sha-chat. l'mon bree-toe ah-sher sohm beeve-sa-ray-noo. Ba-rooch ah-tah Ado-noy, coe-rate ha-breet.
Amidst the following prayer, the baby's name is given: Elo-hey-noo vay-lo-hey ah-vo-tay-noo, ka-yaim eht ha-ye-led ha-zeh l'ah-veev ooh-l'ee-mo, v'yee-ca-rey shmoe b'Yis-ra-ael _____(
say the baby's Hebrew name), bain _____(say the father's
Hebrew name). Yees-moch ha-av b'yo-say cha-la-tzov v'ta-gail ee-mo beef-ree veet-na, ka-ka-toov: Yees-moch ah-vee-cha v'ee'meh-cha, v'ta-gail yoe-lod-te-cha. V'ne-eh-mar: Va-eh-eh-vode ah-la-yeech va-her-aich meet-bo-se-set b'da-ma-yeech, va-oe-mar la'ch b'da-ma-yeech cha-yee, va-owe-mar loch b'da-ma-yeech cha-yee.
V'ne-eh-mar: za-char l'owe-lom bree-toe, da-var tzee-vah l'eh-lef dor. Ah-sher ka-rot eht Av-ra-hom, ooh-sh'voo-ah-toe l'Yeetz-chak, va-ya'mee-de-ha l'Ya-cove l'choke, l'Yis-ra-ail breet owe-lom.

V'ne-eh-mar: va-ya-mahl Av-ra-hom eht Yeetz-chak b'noe ben shmoe-not ya-meem, ka-ah-sher tzee-vah oh-toe Eh-lo-heem. Hoe-dew la-Ado-noy key t'ove, key l'owe-lom chas-doe. Hoe-doe la-Ado-noy key t'ove, key l'oh-lom chas-doe. _____ (say the baby's Hebrew name), bain _____(say the father's Hebrew name), zeh ha-ka-tone ga-dole yee-yeh. K'shame sheh-neech-noss la-breet, cain yee-ca-nais la-breet, cain yee-ca-nais l'Toe-rah, ooh-l'choo-pah, ooh-l'ma-seem toe-veem.

The Pidyan Ha-Ben, The Redemption of the Firstborn Son

Hebrew:

סדר פדיון הבן

הָאָב אוֹמֵר: אִשְׁתִּי הַיִּשְׂרְאֵלִית יָלְדָה לִי בֵּן זֶה הַבְּכוֹר.

הַכֹּהֵן שׁוֹאֵל: מַאי בָּעִית טְפֵי, לִתֵּן לִי בִּנְךָ בְּכוֹרְךָ שֶׁהוּא פֶּטֶר רֶחֶם לְאִמּוֹ, אוֹ בָּעִית לִפְדוֹתוֹ בְּעַד חָמֵשׁ סְלָעִים כִּדְמְחַיְבַתָּא מִדְּאוֹרַיְתָא.

הָאָב מֵשִׁיב: חָפֵץ אֲנִי לִפְדוֹת אֶת בְּנִי, וְהֵא לְךָ דְמֵי פִדְיוֹנוֹ כִּדְמְחַיְבַתִּי מִדְּאוֹרַיְתָא.

הָאָב מֵכִין בְּיָדוֹ אֶת הַכֶּסֶף אוֹ אֶת הַחֵפֶץ לְמָסְרוֹ לַכֹּהֵן וּמְבָרֵךְ:
בָּרוּךְ אַתָּה יְיָ אֱלֹהֵינוּ מֶלֶךְ הָעוֹלָם, אֲשֶׁר קִדְּשָׁנוּ בְּמִצְוֹתָיו, וְצִוָּנוּ עַל פִּדְיוֹן הַבֵּן.
בָּרוּךְ אַתָּה יְיָ אֱלֹהֵינוּ מֶלֶךְ הָעוֹלָם, שֶׁהֶחֱיָנוּ וְקִיְּמָנוּ וְהִגִּיעָנוּ לַזְּמַן הַזֶּה.

הַכֹּהֵן מְקַבֵּל אֶת הַפִּדְיוֹן וְאַחַר כָּךְ נוֹתֵן אֶת יָדוֹ עַל רֹאשׁ הַתִּינוֹק וּמְבָרְכוֹ: יְשִׂמְךָ אֱלֹהִים כְּאֶפְרַיִם וְכִמְנַשֶּׁה. יְבָרֶכְךָ יְיָ וְיִשְׁמְרֶךָ. יָאֵר יְיָ פָּנָיו אֵלֶיךָ וִיחֻנֶּךָּ. יִשָּׂא יְיָ פָּנָיו אֵלֶיךָ וְיָשֵׂם לְךָ שָׁלוֹם. כִּי אֹרֶךְ יָמִים וּשְׁנוֹת חַיִּים וְשָׁלוֹם יוֹסִיפוּ לָךְ. יְיָ יִשְׁמָרְךָ מִכָּל רָע, יִשְׁמֹר אֶת נַפְשֶׁךָ.

וְנוֹטֵל הַכֹּהֵן כּוֹס יַיִן בְּיָדוֹ וּמְבָרֵךְ:
בָּרוּךְ אַתָּה יְיָ אֱלֹהֵינוּ מֶלֶךְ הָעוֹלָם, בּוֹרֵא פְּרִי הַגָּפֶן.

English:
The father says to the kohen: *My wife, an Israelite, has borne me this firstborn son.*

Simply Jewish

The Kohen asks the father: *Which would you prefer, to give me this son, firstborn to his mother, or the five coins that are Biblically required for his redemption?*

Holding the coins the father responds: *I desire to redeem my son, and here is the Biblically required money for his redemption.*

The father hands over the coins to the Kohen and recites:

Blessed are You, Ado-noy, our God, King of the Universe, Who has sanctified us with His commandments, and commanded us concerning the redemption of a son.

Blessed are You, Ado-noy, our God, King of the Universe, Who has granted us life, sustained us and brought us to this occasion.

After accepting the coins the Kohen places his hands on the head of the baby and recites the following blessings:

May God make you like Ephraim and Menasheh.
May Ado-noy bless you and protect you.
May Ado-noy shine His face towards you and show you favor.
May Ado-noy be favorably disposed towards you and grant you peace.
May long days and years of life and peace be added to you.
May Ado-noy guard you against all evil, and guard your soul.
May it be God's will that just as this baby attained redemption, may he also attain Torah knowledge, the wedding canopy, and good deeds. Amen.

The Kohen lifts a glass of wine and recites: *Blessed are You, Ado-noy, our God, King of the Universe, Who creates the fruit of the vine.*

The festive meal follows, it is concluded with the Grace After Meals.

Transliterated:

The father says to the kohen: Eesh-tee ha-Yis-r'ay-leet yal-da lee bain zeh ha-b'chor.

The Kohen asks the father: Mah ba-eet t'fay, lee-tain lee been-cha b'chor-cha sheh-who peh-ter reh-chem l'ee-moe, ooh ba-eet leef-doe-toe b'od cha-maish s'la-eem k'deem-choo-yav-tah mee-d'oh-ray-tah?

Holding the coins the father responds: Cha-faitz ah-nee leef-dowt eht b'nee, v'hay loch d'may feed-yo-no k'deem-choo-yav-tee me'do-rie-ta.

The father hands over the coins to the Kohen and recites:
Ba-rooch ah-tah Ado-noy, Elo-hey-noo meh-lech ha-owe-lom, ah-sher kid-sha-noo b'meetv-voe-tav, v'tzee'va-noo ahl pid-yon ha-bain.

Ba-rooch ah-ta Ado-noy, Elo-hey-noo meh-lech ha-owe-lom, sheh-heh-chee-ya-noo v'kee-ma-noo v'hee-gee-ya-noo lah-zmon hah-zeh.

After accepting the coins the Kohen places his hands on the head of the baby and recites the following blessings:

Y'seem-cha Elo-heem k'Ef-rah-yeem ooh-M'na-sheh.
Y'va-rech-eh-cha Ado-noy v'yeesh-m'reh-chah,
Ya-air Ado-noy pah-nav ay-leh-cha vee-choo-neh-chah,
Yee-sah Ado-noy pah-nav ay-le-cha v'yah-sem l'chah sha-lom.
Key oh-rech ya-meem ooh-sh'note cha-yeem v'sha-lom yo-see-foo loch. Ado-noy yeesh-more eht naf-sheh-cha.

The Kohen lifts a glass of wine and recites:
Ba-rooch ah-tah Ado-noy, Elo-hey-noo meh-lech ha-owe-lom, boe-ray pree ha-ga-fen.

RESOURCE VIII
Recipes

Recipe for Challah

Prep: 1 hour
Cook: 45 to 55 minutes
Rise: 2 hours
Yield: 4 large challahs
          2 ounces active dry yeast + 2 tablespoons sugar
          6 cups warm water, divided
          4 tablespoons kosher salt
          1 (6-pound) bag high-gluten flour
          2 ¼ cups sugar
          4 egg yolks

1 ¼ cups canola oil, divided
2 whole eggs, lightly beaten
½ cup sesame seeds
½ cup poppy seeds

1. In a medium bowl, dissolve yeast and 2 tablespoons of sugar in 2 cups of warm water, cover loosely with a towel and set aside.
2. Place salt in a huge plastic bowl.
3. Add flour to bowl.
4. Add sugar and egg yolks.
5. Yeast should now have bubbled/foamed and doubled in size, if yeast has not bubbled or does not seem active repeat the process again.

6. Make a well in the middle of the flour mixture and slowly pour yeast and sugar water mixture into the well. Then add the remaining 4 cups of warm water into the well. Make sure the water is not too hot. It should be no warmer than you would use for a baby's bath.

7. Start kneading ingredients together and add a ½ cup of oil.

8. For the next 10 to 15 minutes, knead, adding another ½ cup of oil slowly during that time as needed to create a workable dough. Dough shouldn't be too sticky and also should not be dry. It should become one cohesive mass.

9. Loosely cover dough with a large kitchen towel and place in a warm spot in your kitchen for 15 minutes.

10. After 15 minutes, lightly oil your hands and knead again for another 5 minutes adding a touch more oil to the dough if necessary. The dough should now be easier to work with and will become smooth and satiny.

11. Rub a little oil over the top and around the dough. Cover bowl with a kitchen towel. Place covered bowl in a medium plastic garbage bag and place open ends of the bag loosely underneath the bowl, trapping in air.

12. Place in a warm spot and let rise for 1 hour or until doubled in size.

13. Punch dough down and knead (lightly oil your hands if necessary), flipping it and releasing any air bubbles. Cover again, using the towel and the bag, and let rise 1 more hour.

14. Lightly oil your hands, and punch down again. With a sharp knife divide dough into 4 equal parts.

15. Liberally spray 4 (9-inch) round baking pans with non-stick cooking spray and set aside.

16. Preheat oven to 375° F.

For Round Challah

17. With lightly oiled hands, place 1 piece of dough on a smooth work surface. Play with the dough a bit, squeezing out any air bubbles. Then roll the dough into a long, thick rope, adding oil as needed to keep it from being too sticky. Don't use too much oil; a little sticky is fine.

18. Place one end of the rope up against the edge of the prepared pan and coil it, ending in the middle. Set aside.

For Pull-Apart Challah:

19. With lightly oiled hands, place 1 piece of dough on a smooth work surface. Play with the dough a bit, squeezing out any air bubbles. Separate into 8 equal parts. Roll each part into a round ball, adding

oil as needed to keep it from being too sticky. Don't use too much oil; a little sticky is fine.

20. Place one ball in the middle of the prepared pan and surround with remaining balls. Don't worry if they don't touch. They will rise into each other while baking. Set aside.

21. Repeat either method with remaining dough so that you have 4 challahs.

22. Brush challahs with beaten egg and sprinkle with a combination of poppy and sesame seeds.

23. Bake at 375° for 10 minutes and then lower your oven temperature to 350° and bake for an additional 35 to 45 minutes, until challah tops are dark golden brown.

24. Allow to cool slightly before slicing. Serve while still warm. Once the challah has been sliced, you can store the slices in sealable plastic bags for about 4 to 5 days.

Recipe for Chicken Soup

Prep: 15 min
Cook: 1 hr, 45 min
Chill: - Total: 2 hrs
Yield: 6 to 8 servings

Ingredients:

1 (3-1/2-pound) chicken, cut into 8 pieces
12 cups water
1 large carrot, peeled, cut into bite-sized pieces
1 large parsnip, peeled, cut into bite-sized pieces
1 large onion, cut into bite-sized pieces
1 large turnip, peeled, cut into bite-sized pieces
4 medium stalks of celery, cut into bite-sized pieces
3 tablespoons kosher salt
1 (1/2-ounce) chicken consommé stock cube (optional)
1 bouquet garni of 15 parsley sprigs, 15 dill sprigs, 1 tablespoon whole peppercorns
Additional fresh parsley or dill, for garnish (optional)

Preparation:

1. Rinse chicken and place in a 6-quart soup pot.

2. Add water and bring to a boil over high heat. Skim any foam, residue or fat that rises to the surface using a large spoon or skimmer and discard.

3. Once boiling runs clear, reduce heat to a simmer and add carrot, parsnip, onion, turnip, celery and salt. Add stock cube, if desired.

4. Simmer, covered, for 1 hour and 30 minutes.
5. During the last 15 minutes of cooking add the bouquet garni and then remove before serving.
6. Remove chicken from bone and place a few pieces into each bowl. Ladle soup and vegetables over chicken.
7. Mince dill or parsley and sprinkle on immediately before serving, if desired. Or cool the soup and refrigerate overnight.

Recipe for Chulent

Prep: 8 hrs
Cook: overnight
Chill: -
Total: 8 hrs
Yield: 8 servings

Ingredients:

2 medium potatoes, peeled and cut into bite-sized chunks
2 medium onions, cut into bite-sized chunks
1 (2-pound) piece of flanken, cut into 4 to 6 pieces
1/2 tablespoon coarse black pepper
3/4 cup barley
1 cup dried light red kidney beans
3 tablespoons consommé mix
2 tablespoons paprika
2 tablespoons honey
1 (1-pound) kishka loaf
3 cups water

Preparation:

1. Line bottom of slow cooker with potatoes and onions.
2. Rinse flanken and pat dry. Place pieces around sides of crock pot, with bones on the outside.
3. Generously pepper meat.
4. Add barley and beans. Shake the pot a bit so some of the barley and beans fall into the spaces between the potatoes and onions.
5. Season with consommé mix, paprika and honey.
6. Place kishka on top.
7. Pour in water, adding more if necessary, to completely cover all ingredients.
8. Cook on low heat overnight, at least 8 hours.

Links to other 'Quick and Kosher' Recipes and Videos

Gefilte Fish:
www.kosher.com/Recipes/Appetizers/ClassicGefilteFish.html.

Potato Kugel Cups:
www.kosher.com/Recipes/Sides/PotatoKugelCups.html

Honey Chicken:
www.kosher.com/Recipes/Poultry/HoneyChicken.html

Israeli Salad:
www.kosher.com/Recipes/Salads/IsraeliSalad.html.

Sun-dried Tomato Caesar Salad:
www.kosher.com/Recipes/Salads/SunDriedTomatoCaesarSalad.html.

Videos:

Honey Chicken
Cran Apple Crunch Kugel
Spiced Gefilte Fish
http://blog.kosher.com/

Jamie Geller, *Chief Foodie Officer*
VP of Content & Marketing, (as featured on The Early Show, CW11, WABC news and more.)

From Quick & Kosher: Recipes From The Bride Who Knew Nothing, by Jamie Geller, www.quickandkosher.com, and www.kosher.com.

RECOMMENDE'
SOURCES

Recommended Books

- The Artscroll Chumash (Bible), (Artscroll)
- The Complete Artscroll Siddur (prayer book), (transliterated version available), (Artscroll)
- Ethics of the Fathers/Pirkay Avot, I recommend the Artscroll and Rabbi Berel Wein commentaries, (Artscroll, Shaar Press)
- Permission to Believe- Rabbi Leib Kelemen, (Feldheim)
- Permission to Receive- Rabbi Leib Kelemen, (Feldheim)
- To Kindle a Soul- Rabbi Leib Kelemen, (parenting), (Feldheim)
- If You Were God- Rabbi Aryeh Kaplan, (OU/NCSY)
- The Aryeh Kaplen Anthology- Rabbi Aryeh Kaplan, (OU/NCSY)
- Gateway to Judaism- Rabbi Mordechai Becher, (Shaar)
- The Book of Our Heritage- Rabbi Eliyahu Kitov, (Feldheim)
- The Rosh Hashana Survival Kit- Rabbi Shimon Apisdorf, (Leviathan)
- The Passover Survival Kit- Rabbi Shimon Apisdorf, (Leviathan)
- Endless Light- Rabbi David Aaron, (Berkley)
- The Secret Life of God- Rabbi David Aaron, (Isralight)
- The Magic Touch: A Jewish Approach to Relationships- Gila Manolson, (Feldheim)
- The Five Levels of Pleasure- Rabbi Noach Weinberg, (Select Books)
- Tahara Manual of Practices- Rabbi Mosha Epstein (Gross Brothers)
- Remember My Soul- Lori Palatnik, (Khal Publishing)
- The Jewish Way in Death & Mourning- Rabbi Maurice Lamm, (Jonathan David Publishers)
- Soul Searching- Rabbi Yakov Astor, (Targum)
- The Science of God- Dr. Gerald Schroeder, (Broadway Books)
- Quick & Kosher- Jamie Geller, (Feldheim)
- World Perfect- Rabbi Ken Spiro, (Simcha Press)
- The NCSY Bencher, (OU/NCSY)
- Best Names for Jewish Children- Alfred Koltach, (Jonathan David Publishers)

Recommended Websites

- **www.afikimfoundation.org** - The Afikim Foundation is a not-for-profit organization dedicated to furthering Jewish life by developing creative initiatives to meet the critical challenges of our day. Cinema Park-Edutainment, a four hour multi-sensory experience that integrates 3D projection, interactive wireless remotes, laser lighting and special effects, and transports viewers in the course of moments, into the human body, mind and soul as it explores the uniqueness of man; The portable "One Soul Holocaust Educational Exhibit"; and books like this one, are some examples of Afikim projects.

- **www.aish.com** - "Since its launch in February 2000, Aish.com has become the world's largest Jewish content website, logging over a million monthly user sessions with 380,000 unique email subscribers, publishing over 10,000 articles -- on career, dating, parenting, spirituality, Israel events -- offering "wisdom for living" for the modern world. Aish.com's goal is to give every Jew the opportunity to discover their heritage in an atmosphere of open inquiry and mutual respect." Additionally, Aish offers educational programming in many cities in the United States and internationally. The main location is in Jerusalem, near the Western Wall.

- **www.chabad.org** - Chabad-Lubovitch, widely known for the exceptionally friendly "Chabad Houses" that are open to Jews of all backgrounds, also offers a website that provides a wide amount of helpful information. Their mission is to "utilize internet technology to unite Jewry worldwide, empower them with knowledge of their 3,300 year-old tradition, and foster within them a deeper connection to Judaism's rituals and faith.

- **www.discoveryproduction.com** - Discovery. If you could only attend one seminar, this is the one I would recommend. "Discovery packs the wisdom and relevance of Jewish values and ideas into a spectacular and moving demonstration of the case for Judaism, inviting participants to challenge Judaism's central principles in a novel process called Failsafe. Based on analytical techniques used by the Mossad, the Israeli intelligence agency, this chain of discussions draws audiences into a fascinating and rigorously intellectual means of testing the rational basis for belief in Judaism. Through the warm, entertaining and non-judgmental atmosphere, audiences discover that Judaism has the tools for enhancing one's self-esteem, personal power and enjoyment of life."

- **www.gatewaysonline.com** - The Gateways mission is to "empower Jews of all ages to unlock the treasure of their heritage. Dedicated to ensuring a vibrant Jewish future, our immersion learning approach enables Jews of all backgrounds to engage the richness of Jewish values and traditions while building and reinforcing their bond with the Jewish people and Israel." Gateways provides excellent weekend retreats and holiday seminars for Jews of all backgrounds and levels of observance. The seminars feature top notch speakers and excellent hotel accommodations.

- **www.isralight.org** - Isralight is "dedicated to inspiring a worldwide Jewish renaissance through essential and innovative educational solutions that empower Jews to experience the relevance, wisdom and joy of Jewish living." Fair enough, but I want to add as an attendee of more than one spiritual retreat, I know that Isralight offers the opportunity to experience Jewish wisdom in an inclusive, warm, welcoming and non-judgmental atmosphere. The main location is in Jerusalem, near the Western Wall, but retreats and classes are offered in the Unites States periodically.

- **www.jewsforjudiasm.com** - Jews for Judaism's mission is to "strengthen and preserve Jewish identity through education and counseling that counteracts deceptive proselytizing targeting Jews for conversion."

- **www.ohr.edu** Ohr Samayach - "Educating Jews whom no synagogue or movement will ever find." Ohr Somayach, gives young adults "searching for their roots a chance to experience Jewish learning in their own language, at their own pace and at an intellectual level that rivals and surpasses that of the Ivy League universities from which many have come."

- **www.partnersintorah.org** - Partners in Torah pairs up Jewish adults who want to learn more about Judaism with a volunteer mentor for weekly Jewish study, usually via telephone. The program provides an incredible opportunity to study anything you like, from the comfort of your own home free of charge. As a long time mentor I strongly recommend this program!

ABOUT THE AUTHOR

He is known as "Rabbi Reuven," and in addition to being an avid runner currently preparing for the New York Marathon, he has been practicing law for over two decades, and been involved in Jewish education for many years. Rabbi Reuven has served as the Director of the Rockland Outreach Center, Principal of the Total Hebrew School and leads Birthright trips to Israel.

He lives in New York with his wife Susan and their five wonderful children. Reuven and Susan enjoy sharing their family Shabbat experience with guests, and are happy to host people who wish to experience Shabbat. Rabbi Reuven is a popular speaker and frequent guest lecturer for numerous organizations.

He can be reached at reuvenepstein@aol.com.